MAUREEN MAGUIRE was [illegible] travelled widely and has live[illegible] K and Germany. She has a PhD in H[illegible] mic Research from the University of Glasgow.

She has worked as a teacher at schools and [illegible] nd is involved in voluntary youth work. Maureen is marri[illegible] Jan Bruns, a television cameraman, and they currently live in Germany with their two teenage children, Christina and Mark.

In 1992 she published *Less Than Complete*, a volume of poems by Philip Padfield, a British hostage held in Beirut and killed by his captors. Maureen was moved to bring to public attention the plight of young women prisoners when her sister, Maria McGuire, Advocate, represented the family of one of the dead girls at the Fatal Accident Inquiry into three suicides at Cornton Vale Prison.

[Un]comfortably Numb

A Prison Requiem

MAUREEN MAGUIRE

Luath Press Limited

EDINBURGH

www.luath.co.uk

First published 2001

The paper used in this book is acid-free, neutral-sized and recyclable.
It is made from low chlorine pulps produced in a low energy,
low emission manner from sustainable forests.

Printed and bound by
Bell & Bain Ltd., Glasgow

Designed by Tom Bee

Typeset in 10.5 point Sabon by
S. Fairgrieve, Edinburgh 0131 658 1763

for

Kelly	†23.06.1995,
Arlene	†26.06.1995,
Joanna	†03.12.1995,
Angela	†26.04.1996,
Denise	†03.09.1996,
Yvonne	†24.12.1996,
Sandra	†03.12.1997,
Mary	†04.07.1998

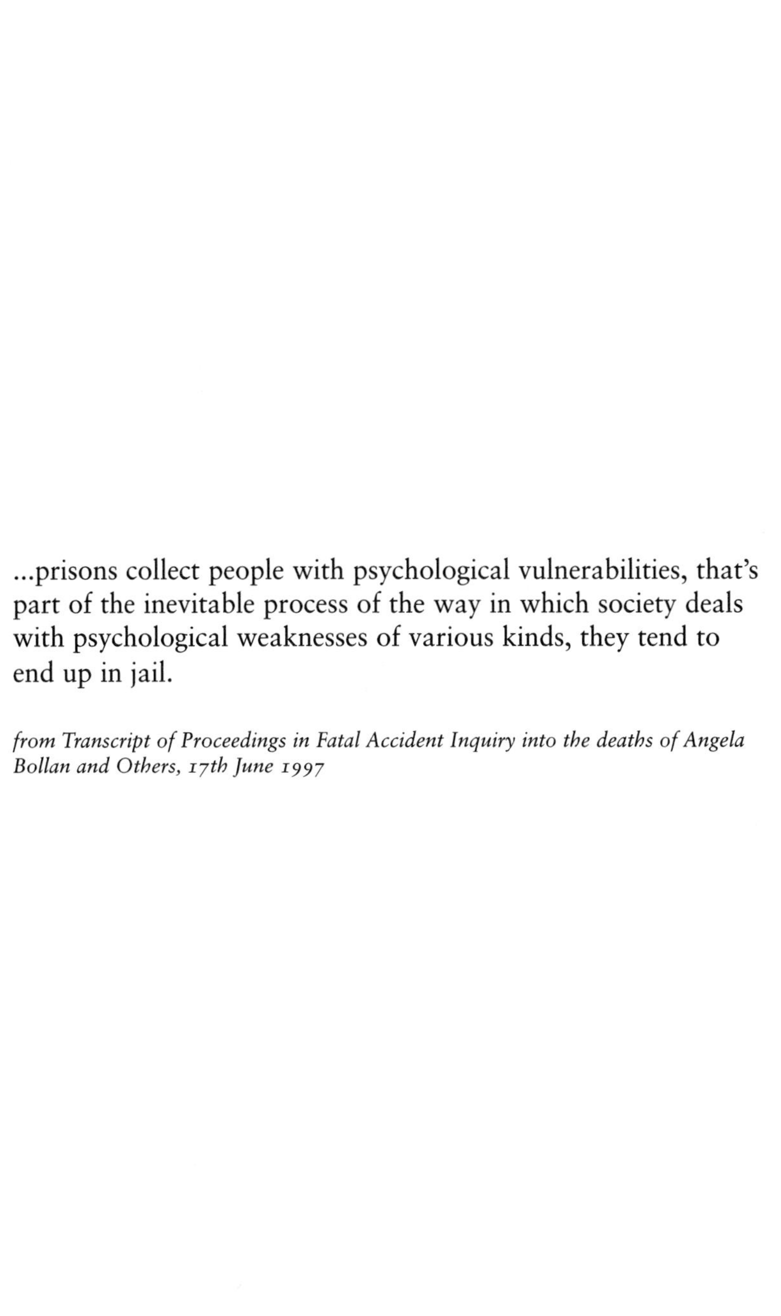

...prisons collect people with psychological vulnerabilities, that's part of the inevitable process of the way in which society deals with psychological weaknesses of various kinds, they tend to end up in jail.

from Transcript of Proceedings in Fatal Accident Inquiry into the deaths of Angela Bollan and Others, 17th June 1997

Contents

Foreword

I remember it was over a holiday weekend that Yvonne Gilmour's dad called me to ask if I would advise him on a case coming up to do with his daughter. He said little more until we met at my office, and he then gave me the beginnings of the tragedy of his daughter's death in Cornton Vale Prison. The suicides had been in the news for some time, and I was asked to represent Mr Gilmour in the forthcoming Fatal Accident Inquiry at Stirling Sheriff Court, which was to be a composite FAI, also dealing with two other suicides at the prison.

We were only days away from the start of the hearing, and a great many preparations and personnel were to be dealt with. The work was done. Maria Maguire, our counsel, and I made ourselves ready for the case and, along with the other legal teams and lay persons in court, we sat through many days and weeks of testimony from witnesses from various backgrounds, mainly professional or fellow inmates. I was able to read copious statements, reports and documents by all the officials and prisoners involved in Cornton Vale life, and, of course, death. As a solicitor of twenty years practice, I was aware of the lot of prisoners, male and female, and I was no stranger to visiting the Vale.

But the case of Yvonne Gilmour has shown me a deeper, more intimate, and more authoritative image of female incarceration. If I was sympathetic before, now I am wholly on the side of the overwhelming majority of girls in prison. I simply believe they should not be there. With a tiny number of exceptions, women who find themselves behind the bars of Cornton Vale, probably any women's prison, are victims rather than candidates for punishment alone. Whether through drugs, poverty, prostitution or more likely a combination of these and other social and domestic factors, these are people who have failed the test of society, missed out on the gifts to enjoy what most of us take for granted, or been deprived of weapons to fight for an acceptable, let alone an easy, life.

That so many girls find a path through prison without recourse to self-harm is testament to the human spirit. That so many fail to find the path is a mainly untold and unrecognised story. For every Yvonne Gilmour who dies, there are dozens at least, maybe more, who live and suffer in silence, depression and fear.

I always thought prison was at worst to punish humanely, and at best to rehabilitate. I am afraid that in our society, prison does little more for many women than to clean them temporarily of habitual drug-taking and keep them from a chaotic lifestyle for a while, to release them back to life no better than they left on conviction. Yvonne needed help, and hope. The staff and management of the prison did their job, for better or worse. The responsibility is with all of us, as governors, politicians, voters, citizens, to distinguish between law, justice and mercy. To do that, we need to learn and understand how prison and prisoners work. We then need to turn from retribution to recognition and rehabilitation. It is a crucial test.

[Un]comfortably Numb is not a legal textbook or jurisprudential treatise, although it should be read by every criminal lawyer, prosecutor, judge and law-maker. Essentially it is an investigation into something our sophisticated society can't easily face, and has to hide away behind bars and walls. Society created these tragedies, and this book challenges us all to recognise that, and do something about it.

Austin Lafferty

Preface

This is the story of Yvonne Gilmour, a young woman who took her own life one Christmas Eve in Cornton Vale Prison. She was the sixth inmate to hang herself in the prison in the space of eighteen months. Two more would follow. At least four more incidents could have been fatal if staff had not intervened in time.

None of these young women was facing a long sentence and most of them were on remand. Some of them would have been released in a matter of weeks. Several of them had children. Was the prison so bad that it drove its inmates to suicide? Was the Prison Medical Officer right when he said that the prison was not a hellish place but it was hellish for the girls being there?

Society tried to find answers. The deaths were duly investigated by Fatal Accident Inquiries, which heard months of evidence from prison staff, prisoners, experts, and family members. Such Inquiries are seen to have two essential purposes: 'the enlightenment of those legitimately interested in the death (i.e. relatives and dependents) of the deceased as to the circumstances of death ... and the enlightenment of the public at large as to whether any reasonable steps could or should have been taken whereby the death might have been avoided.' Although the Inquiries were open to the public, little of their efforts reached the public ear except when journalists saw fit to report on the evidence of the day. The Inquiries resulted in Sheriff determinations as to the cause of death (suicide) but made no determinations in terms of the Fatal Accidents and Sudden Deaths Inquiry (Scotland) Act 1976 Section 6(1)(c), which deals with any reasonable precautions whereby the death(s) might have been avoided, or (d) which refers to any defects in any system which contributed to the death(s). Several suggestions for improvements within the prison were made.

Society had done its duty in investigating the circumstances of the girls' deaths. Public opinion granted that the suicides were a tragedy but because they happened behind bars, it was the Prison Service's problem. But is it?

Britain has one of the highest suicide rates in Europe. There is one suicide every 79 minutes. Many of these are young people. Each day two people under the age of 24 kill themselves in Britain. Suicide accounts for almost 20% of all deaths of young people in Britain.

Scotland's suicide rate is the highest in the UK, 50 per cent higher than that of the UK as a whole in 1994-96. According to statistics issued by the Samaritans, 878 took their own lives in Scotland in 1998, a 13% rise over a period of ten years. The most dramatic, and unexplained, increase has been amongst younger people, especially young males. A recent report, *The Sorrows of Young Men: Exploring the Increasing Risk of Suicide*, published by the Edinburgh University Centre for Theology and Public Issues (September 2000) revealed that the third most frequent cause of death among young Scots was now suicide. In the 15-24 age group suicide accounts for almost one in five deaths, a rise of almost 150% for males since the 1970s (taking over from road accidents as the number one cause of death for young adult males) and almost 120% for females.

Behind bars, young prisoners represent the largest group of at-risk individuals, particularly those under 21 who make up a substantial proportion of the remand population. In 1998, 21% of prison suicides were by people 21 or under.

The percentage of suicides in prison is much higher than in the population at large. Based on figures for 1995 comparing suicide rates in 14 European prison systems, Scotland headed the table with 284 deaths per 100,000 inmates, almost 100 more than the next listed. Prison suicides are increasing, disproportionate to the rise in the prison population. Between 1995 and 1996, the rate of suicides in prison increased by 106% while the average daily prison population increased by only 4%. With 80 inmates having killed themselves in Scottish prisons since 1992, the death rate is now almost twice that of prisons in England. Most of these have been males. 39 prisoners have killed themselves in Barlinnie Prison since 1986, and since 1992 there have been 14 confirmed suicides at Greenock Prison, many of them, as in Cornton Vale, involving remand prisoners. Between 1976 and 1994 only 1 of the 83 suicides in Scottish prisons was by a female prisoner. By 1995, 3 of the 8 suicides in Scottish prisons were female prisoners, although women accounted for only 3% of the average daily prison population. Since Cornton Vale houses 96% of women prisoners in Scotland (there are facilities for holding small numbers of women prisoners in Aberdeen, Inverness and Dumfries), it is there that the deaths have occurred. The rate of suicides at Cornton Vale is higher than at Holloway Prison (5 suicides between 1992 and 1997) although Cornton Vale's average daily population (under 200) is less than half that of Holloway's (500).

Scotland's Chief Inspector of Prisons has attributed the country's 'disproportionate rise in prison suicides' to drink and drug addictions. Drug offences increased by 109% between 1985 and 1995. Almost 90% of women in Cornton Vale have had some experience of illicit drug use, with heroin the main drug of choice. In 1999 figures released at a conference in London called *The Crisis in Women's Prisons* show that a third of women had been imprisoned for drug offences and another third for drug-related incidents. Should these women be in prison?

In the course of the 20th century, the number of women being sent to prison dropped so much that the Government was led to comment in 1979, 'It may well be that as the end of the century draws nearer, penological progress will result in even fewer or no women at all being given prison sentences.' Such optimism was short-lived. By mid-1999 the number of women in British prisons had reached record levels. According to *The Crisis in Women's Prisons* the number of women behind bars in 1998 had doubled in five years to 3,105. In Scotland there has been a steady increase in female prisoners since 1991, reaching a record of 220 late 1999. A review commissioned by the Scottish Office Minister for Home Affairs after the seventh suicide in Cornton Vale published its findings in 1998 (*Women Offenders – A Safer Way*). One of its conclusions was that the number of women offenders being sent to prison could and should be reduced. According to SACRO (Safeguarding Communities, Reducing Offending in Scotland), the prisoners' support group, Scotland is still sending more people to prison than any other European country except Portugal.

Like Yvonne Gilmour and the other girls who died in Cornton Vale, most of these women are not criminals. Less than 1% of female convictions are for violent crime. Women are most likely to be convicted for failure to pay for a TV licence, shoplifting, breach of the peace, and speeding. Up to 52% of female prison-sentenced admissions are fine defaulters, most of these in connection with soliciting for prostitution. Women represent almost all the convictions relating to prostitution and they are much more likely than men to be convicted for failing to send their children to school, or for social security fraud. Women are also disproportionately represented in all convictions for failure to appear at court. (Men, on the other hand, are disproportionately represented in crimes of violence and indecency.) The majority of women prisoners are parents separated from their children. About 70% have at least one child.

A substantial amount of women in custody, well over a third according to one survey, have attempted to take their own lives at some point, usually outside of prison. There are many reasons why people try to commit suicide. Canadian research, published in 2000, has claimed to have discovered a gene which may predispose people to suicide, but this ignores important exacerbating factors such as poverty, deprivation, mental illness, drug and alcohol addiction, broken families and relationships, or negative childhood experiences. A high proportion of women offenders suffer from a history of emotional, physical and sexual abuse. In one survey, 82% had experienced some form of abuse during their lives. Sexual abuse was frequent, most commonly during childhood on a regular basis from fathers or other male relatives or guardians.

Suicide is a topic of conversation in prison. It is, as it were, in the air, like a virus. Richard Dawkin's theory of cultural transmission, originally described in 1976 (*The Selfish Gene*), has found application in several areas. Dawkins coined the term *meme* to describe a unit of cultural transmission, examples of which would be 'tunes, ideas, catch-phrases, clothes, fashions...' which propagate themselves by 'leaping from brain to brain via a process, which, in the broad sense, can be called imitation'. Perhaps suicide has become a prison *meme*. The majority of women in Cornton Vale are very young and therefore vulnerable to such 'viruses'. Although young people under the age of 16 are diverted from the adult courts to the Children's Hearings Systems as much as possible, imprisonment begins early for many, some experiencing custody at age 15. A fifth of Cornton Vale inmates are under the age of 21, two-thirds under the age of 30.

Yvonne Gilmour was one of these vulnerable young women. She and the other girls who took their lives in Cornton Vale ended up behind bars because society had nowhere else to put them. What they needed was not custody but help with their drug problem and with the deep-rooted traumas that were causing them to escape into drugs. Their stories have much in common. They had been using drugs or alcohol or both from an early age to escape a reality they could not cope with. The more they abused drugs, the more reality became impossible for them. Most of them had tried methadone stabilisation and detoxification programmes. They had lived in supervised hostels and rehabilitation centres. Some of them had very supportive families. In order to feed their drug habit, they became involved in petty crime – and were sent to prison. They could not cope with prison life, with withdrawal from drugs, with their problems. They saw suicide as a solution, the only solution, the final solution.

The deaths of the young women have led to some reforms in Cornton Vale. The Scottish Prison Service has supported or initiated research, most notably Dr Nancy Louks' research into drugs, alcohol, bullying and suicide at Cornton Vale (1998) and the review *Women Offenders – A Safer Way* already quoted. As a result of the latter, an Inter-Agency Forum was set up in Glasgow to examine community-based criminal justice services for women, including bail, as an alternative to prison custody. In Cornton Vale itself, there is an attempt to emphasise care as well as custody, especially for remand and short-term inmates, addicted prisoners and those at risk of suicide. But such reforms, commendable as they are, do not solve the problem. In the 1999-2000 Annual Report of the Scottish Prison Service, 13 prison officers were listed as having received commendations for preventing attempted suicides in Scottish prisons, including Cornton Vale. What is needed for these vulnerable girls, as research and experience have been indicating, is an alternative to prison. And we have to ask different questions. Why is it that so many of our young people in the past two decades have turned to drugs? What is it about society that makes them want to escape it? Where have we failed them? If we are to learn from the deaths of these young people, those are the questions we must start with. The Chief Inspector of England and Wales entitled his recent report on reducing suicides in prison *Suicide is Everyone's Concern*, most appropriate in light of the fact that, statistically speaking, one in four of us knows someone personally who committed suicide. Suicide *is* our concern.

[Un]comfortably Numb is a documentary presentation based largely on the Fatal Accident Inquiry which investigated the fourth, fifth and sixth suicides. This was a particularly extensive Inquiry, one of the longest-running in Scottish legal history, which heard 33 days of evidence in March and June 1997. I have chosen to tell the story in the words of those involved

because it is the nearest we can come to what Yvonne and the other girls lived through. It is the nearest the dead girls can come to telling their own stories. Although the presentation focuses on Yvonne Gilmour, her story represents the plight of all eight girls who died in Cornton Vale, of those who have attempted suicide behind bars and those who still do, and of the many young girls who have taken their lives outside prison. There are more similarities in the circumstances of their lives and deaths than differences.

Maureen Maguire

Acknowledgements

I would like to thank Yvonne Gilmour's father, Richard Gilmour, and her sisters, Michelle and Carolann, for their kind permission to tell Yvonne's story and for their courage in allowing it to be told openly. It is their hope that it will help to prevent other families from losing their daughters, sisters or mothers so needlessly.

My thanks also to their solicitor, Austin Lafferty, who kindly allowed me access to his Fatal Accident Inquiry material and who was supportive of the project from the start.

R.A. Dunlop, QC, Sheriff Principal of Tayside, Central and Fife was very helpful in the matter of legal permission to use the material quoted. I am grateful to Scottish Court Service for granting permisssion to quote from the transcripts of the Fatal Accident Inquiry.

My thanks also go to Governor Kate Donegan, who, at a time of unsettlement due to recent suicides, took time to show me round Cornton Vale Prison and answer my questions.

Without the help of my sister Maria Maguire, Advocate, this book might never have seen successful completion. She guided me through the legal intricacies, and her commitment to the project provided invaluable help and encouragement.

Prologue:
Death Behind Bars

†23 June 1995

KELLY HOLLAND, aged 17, was arrested in the early hours of 21 June 1995 on charges of breach of the peace and resisting arrest. She appeared at Court on the morning of the next day and was remanded in custody for trial.

The prison officer spoke to various prisoners in their cells in the course of his rounds. Gradually the girls began to go to sleep. ... He checked Kelly Holland at the appropriate intervals. He spoke to her twice. Once about 9.45p.m. when he asked her how she was getting on, she said 'Fine'. He spoke again about 11.00p.m. and made some reference to her getting out into the sun in the morning. She replied, 'Yeah, I will.' He noted that she was writing a letter at one stage. He also said that her eyes were red as if she had been crying. When he checked her at 12.45a.m. and saw her hanging from the window with a ligature round her neck, he broke out his emergency key and rushed in. He took the weight of her body for a short time while radioing for assistance.

Given the evidence of the Pathologist that a matter of two minutes would be sufficient for death to ensue after the fixing of the ligature, it is clear that Kelly Holland had ample time to arrange the ligature and bring about her own death between the points of observation (by prison staff). I do not consider that I can fault the system with regard to that.

Determination by John Joseph Maguire, Queen's Counsel, Sheriff Principal of the Sheriffdom of Tayside Central and Fife in the Fatal Accident Inquiry into the deaths of Kelly Holland and Arlene Elliott, 8th March 1996

†26 June 1995

ARLENE ELLIOT, aged 17, was imprisoned on May 30, 1995 on charges of theft.

Arlene Elliot was clearly a person of considerable vulnerability.

After the death of Kelly Holland there was a degree of tension in the Prison. The staff were concerned and vigilant. The inmates were disturbed. Arlene Elliot had been placed on Strict Suicide Supervision on the Friday morning, removed from there later in the day and was taken off observation on the Saturday. She was then in the mainstream of the Prison. A number of staff and prisoners gave evidence that that she seemed happier during that period. She was relieved not to be on Strict Suicide Supervision.

One witness said that Arlene Elliot was speaking about Kelly Holland a lot. There was some suggestion that it should not have been Kelly but her.

The last occasion Arlene Elliot was seen was in the sitting room sometime before she went to her cell. She indicated she was going for a bath and then for a sleep. Her cell mate thought she was 'brand new' after the dosage of Largactil had been reduced. A prison officer who was in the sitting room on the Sunday evening says she last saw Arlene Elliot about 7.10p.m. At 7.20p.m. she decided to go and look for her but was diverted. At 7.30p.m. some inmates came across Arlene Elliot hanging in her cell.

Determination by John Joseph Maguire, Queen's Counsel, Sheriff Principal of the Sheriffdom of Tayside Central and Fife in the Fatal Accident Inquiry into the deaths of Kelly Holland and Arlene Elliot, 8th March 1996

†3 December 1995

JOANNA O'REILLY, age 26, had been released on bail for reports. Having failed to make herself available for a Social Work report for the Court, a warrant was issued and she was arrested on Wednesday, 29 November. She appeared at Glasgow District Court on 30 November and was remanded to HM Prison, Cornton Vale.

I move on now to the final hours of Miss O'Reilly's life. The inmates were locked up at about 5p.m. They were given tea between 6.05 and 6.15p.m. About the same time those who required medication were released, given their medication and returned to their cells. This finished about 6.30p.m. Thereafter it was the duty of two officers to do observations. They said they did these. A number of inmates said that no observations were done until the 'goodnight check' during which Miss O'Reilly was found to be hanging in her cell.

There was much confusion with regard to timing. This is almost inevitable as the finding of Miss O'Reilly's body was a considerable shock to the two officers and indeed to the prisoners. They heard Officers at the door. Some saw Miss O'Reilly in silhouette at the window. The inmates started screaming and shouting and ringing their alarm bells...

Determination by John Joseph Maguire, Queen's Counsel, Sheriff Principal of the Sheriffdom of Tayside Central and Fife in the Fatal Accident Inquiry into the death of Joanna May O'Reilly, 6th September, 1996

†26 April 1996

ANGELA BOLLAN, aged 19, was arrested on a charge of shoplifting on 12 April 1996 and remanded to HM Prison Cornton Vale. She allegedly stole 8 packets of Gillette Contour razor blades, 15 bottles of Cloister body spray cans and 4 bottles of Impulse body spray.

FATAL ACCIDENT INQUIRY

Now, I'm sorry if this is going to be distressing for you, but can you tell us what you noticed about Angela at that time in terms of her appearance?

When I first went into the room and seen Angela I thought she was fitting, and then I realised that Mr Taylor wouldn't be holding her against the wall if she was fitting. And then it wasn't until I looked again that I seen the sheets hanging to the bars on the window and it was tied round her neck.

So, you could see a sheet which was tied to the bars of the window and round her neck?

Yes.

Do you remember which part of the bars the sheet was tied to?

The top of the bars.

The top of the bars?

Uh huh.

Did you notice anything about Angela's face at all?

Yes, it was discoloured.

I'm sorry?

It was discoloured.

It was discoloured?

Yes, there was no colour in her face.

Did she appear to be conscious?

I don't know.

Did you notice anything else about her face apart from the colour?

Her eyes, I couldn't see the coloured bits of her eyes.

You couldn't see the coloured bits of her eyes?
[inaudible] and there was foam coming out of her mouth.

Foam?
Uh huh.

Did you say anything when you entered the cell and saw this?
No, I didn't ...

I'm sorry?
I didn't say anything.

Did Mr Taylor say anything?
Mr Taylor said, 'get help'.

Cornton Vale inmate. Transcript of Proceedings in Fatal Accident Inquiry into the death of Angela Bollan and Others, 11th March 1997

You heard Mr Taylor screaming?
I heard him shouting for help.

What did you do?
I ran to Angela's cell.

I take it then you obviously left your own cell. Did you go right into Angela's cell?
Uh huh.

And who was there?
Mr Taylor.

Anyone else?
Angela.

And where was she?
She was hanging from the curtains.

What was Mr Taylor doing?
He was holding her up, trying to stop her frae getting strangled.

What did you do when you saw that, do you remember?
Collapsed.

Did you pass out?
Yes.

Cornton Vale inmate. Transcript of Proceedings in Fatal Accident Inquiry into the death of Angela Bollan and Others, 17th March 1997

Miss White, the officer, came back in the living-room wi' tea an' aw that an' sat us all doon, gave us tobacco an' aw that, and sat us aw doon. We wis aw in a terrible state but wan lassie wis in shock, she wis hysterical, Miss White couldnae calm her doon. Miss White's sitting wi us for ages an' it wis jist dead quiet, everybody wis was jist aw sittin' dead quiet, greetin'. Then Miss White kept goin' oot and men officers were comin' in an' talking to her an' we wur still aw sittin' quiet. She came back in and says we've got her pulse back, an' we wir aw hopin' an' hopin'. She went back oot tae see how things were goin' an' she wis tryin' tae keep everybody the gether 'cause we wir aw, we wir aw hysterical, an' then she came back in an' says we've lost her.

Cornton Vale inmate. Transcript of Proceedings in Fatal Accident Inquiry into the death of Angela Bollan and Others, 7th March 1997

†3 September 1996

DENISE DEVINE, aged 26, was charged on 19 August 1996 under the Carrying of Knives (Scotland) Act 1993 Section 1 (1) and the Bail Etc. (Scotland) Act 1980 Section 3(1) (b).

FATAL ACCIDENT INQUIRY

Now, am I right in thinking that the first duties of the incoming early shift are to check the numbers of inmates and to manually lock the doors prior to them being electronically unlocked?

That's correct, sir, yes.

Now did you take part in that procedure that morning?

No, sir.

Did you have occasion to go to Denise Devine's cell some time during the course of that morning shift?

Yes, sir.

What time was that?

It was approximately ten past seven in the morning.

And why were you going to her cell at that stage?

I was going to her cell at that stage to open her up, to let her out to make the breakfast and to get her medication.

Do I take it that the numbers check and the electronic unlocking of all the cells would have taken place at some stage prior to that?

Yes, indeed, sir.

So it would be necessary for you to unlock the door manually for her to get out of the cell?

Yes, sir.

Can you tell us what you actually did when you went to the cell door?

When I went to her door I unlocked her door and I have like a small ritual where I would give a tap, either on the wooden door or the metal plate, because it makes a louder noise, and that's to alert any prisoners behind the door that I'm coming through. I would be talking on the way through, maybe saying good morning, so they know it is a male member of staff that is coming through their door. On opening Denise's door I noticed that her light was off, so it just makes you that wee bit more wary, you know, that she's maybe not up. On opening the door, I seen Denise, she appeared to be in a sitting position just behind the door, and then I seen the sheet tied from the top of the bunk round her neck.

Now, you told us that you initially went out of the cell briefly to pass a message to your colleague and then came back in?

Yes.

And I think you mentioned that you went over and lifted Denise at that stage?

Uh huh.

Can you tell us whether or not the weight of her body was being borne by the ligature at the time that you lifted her?

No, I can't tell.

Is it possible that it was?

Yes.

Is it possible also that there was some slack in the sheet between where it was tied to the bed and where it was attached to her?

No, there was no slack. I mean the sheet was coming down quite tight and it was against the bars. I mean, it wasn't lying slack in any way at all.

But you can't say whether her full weight was being borne by it, is that fair?

Yes.

Were you able to tell at the stage where you lifted her whether in fact her bottom or her legs had been touching the floor?

Her feet were touching the floor because when I lifted her up she appeared to be dead light and then it dawned on me later that I had been pulling against her legs and I had maybe lifted her up levering her on her legs.

Whereabouts was the sheet, or which part of her body was the sheet attached to?

It was tied round her neck.

Was there a knot?

There was a knot.

Did you notice anything about her appearance, her facial appearance I mean, at that stage?

No, all that I noticed was that she was very pale, and when I lifted her up there was no heat in her at all. I tried to avoid looking at her face, so more or less the only impression I got was it was white and there was a dark bit around about her mouth.

Was there anything else noticeable about her body when you touched her?

Not until I put her down. I mean, nothing I was doing seemed to make sense. Before I had been told that if anybody lifts someone up, it's like a dead weight and it's really difficult to get the knot untied. That wasn't the case for me, and it wasn't until I had actually got her down on the ground that I noticed that she was fairly stiff. Her arm was protruding, when I was lying her down, her arm was protruding, it was more or less above her stomach, and I can't remember what her other arm was doing, more or less what it is doing in the photograph there. Again it was off the floor and very rigid.

So there was a stiffness about her limbs and did that indicate to you that rigor mortis may have set in?

Yes, sir, uh huh.

Did you form any impression then about her condition, her general condition at that stage?

Yes, I'd say it was then that I knew that she was dead and there was nothing at all that could be done.

Cornton Vale Prison Officer. Transcript of Proceedings in Fatal Accident Inquiry into the death of Angela Bollan and Others, 19th March 1997

†24.12.1996

PART ONE

Family Life

CHAPTER I

A Father's Daughter

I wasn't married to Yvonne's mother but we had three children together, three lassies. She went off with Yvonne and her sisters when Yvonne was about 8 weeks old. The other two were about 2 and 4. She went to her sister who was what you'd call a lady of business in Leicester. I came home from work one night and found that she'd cleared the house and taken the children with her.

The Social wouldn't tell me where they were but I was worried about my lassies and I persisted. Their mother had taken the DSS books with her so I thought they could provide an address for me when she made a claim down south. But they said that was confidential. I told them I knew her sister was, you know, a lady of business and that she herself used to be one too until I met her so you can imagine I was worried my girls would come to moral harm. In the end, one of the Social Workers told me where to find them. He said they were living in a ghetto in Leicester where they took a dim view of outsiders and it would be dangerous to go there.

I took the overnight train, the one that got in at seven in the morning. The address was in a black area. I knocked on the door and a woman I'd never seen before let me in. I went up the stairs and found their mother lying out for the count with drink or drugs on a settee. I saw Michelle and Carolann lying on a bed in a press recess, both of them looking as if they had been ill-treated. Carolann's nappy had not been changed for a while and they were upset. I found Yvonne lying in her pram in the kitchen. A beer bottle with a dummy tit on it was lying beside her. Then this coloured chap came out stark naked. I couldn't believe he would walk about like that in front of the kids and I went for him. The girls screamed. I went for someone else as well. Someone called the police and I was taken to the station.

I told the police what I was doing but they just said I can't come down there and take the law into my own hands and they put me back on a train to Glasgow.

But I went back again, this time with my brother as back-up and I more or less raided the house. I found the children much as I had left them two weeks before. They were in their night clothes. I told her to pack some bags with their things. On the train a couple of old ladies helped me to get them changed and cleaned up a bit. One of them was being met by someone in a van and he gave us a lift home.

I contacted the Social and had the girls checked at the clinic. Their backsides were in a terrible state with not having their nappies changed. The clinic gave me cream and stuff. They said there was common hygiene neglect but nothing of a serious nature wrong with them.

I took leave of absence from work for two weeks to get the girls fixed up in a children's home because obviously I couldn't look after them on my own if I was working. I had free access and could see them as and when I wanted. I contacted a solicitor and got full custody. There were no objections from their mother. We were together a lot, weekends, holidays and if I had early shift.

Eventually, the Social Work told me that because of cutbacks I would have to put the children to foster carers or look after them myself. I took early redundancy from the steel works so as I could be with the kids. We had two years together. We lived in Dalmarnock. They were wonderful years. They really were. The girls went to school, at least the older two did. I did all the things they'd missed – baptism, First Holy Communion. Because they were wee girls, they needed a lot of nice things. I wanted them to look nice. I had to buy a lot. I was a single father but didn't get much support. The amount of money I got from redundancy the Social wouldn't give me any assistance in any other way to help, and over that period of two years I was getting 21 pounds from the broo. Once my money started going down I asked to get assistance and they said I didn't qualify for anything like that. Their mother was still cashing their family allowance and it took a while for me to get it transferred to me. It was 3 pounds each. My family helped out, especially my mother. But money was tight and the girls were getting older.

Then I did the stupidest thing. I asked the girls' gran to contact their mother to see if she would take them for a month or so until I found a job. I sent them all back down south, and it's something I regret to this day. After a month or two I found a job on the railway. I started off washing the trains. So once I had the job and was earning a decent wage I tried to get the girls back but their mother had moved to another area and I couldn't find out where they were. It was a couple of years later I found out she had split the girls up.

Michelle had been sent to Nottingham with friends of her mother because she had seen her mother being stabbed. Carolann had been put in a children's home. Yvonne was still with her mother. Her mother was still a prostitute and was involved in drinking and drug-taking so Yvonne was in the middle of all that. Her mother had a boy with a coloured chap and he stayed with them too.

I didn't see my children for years, despite repeated attempts to get in touch with them. It was Carolann who got in touch with me in the end and I went down to see her. She was staying in a foster home with a Jamaican family. They were getting 30 to 50 pounds a week to look after her. Other people were getting money to look after my girls but I had to go before a Board to prove myself. I tried to get her back but the Social Work there wouldn't allow me to take her back. Carolann took me to see Yvonne. She would have been about seven then. But I lost touch with Yvonne after that. It was about ten years before I saw her again. I went down to see Michelle after I found out where she was and Carolann and Yvonne were waiting for me coming off the train. After that I was up and down for different things, when Yvonne was in prison, when Carolann had the grandchild. Eventually, I got them all houses up here.

Carolann was the first. Then Michelle, who had a baby in

Nottingham, came up too. Yvonne phoned as well and said, 'Dad, can I come home'. And I said, 'course you can'. She said, 'I want to be with my family'. I broke down in tears. I'd got my lassies back.

We're a great family now, with the grandchildren. We're all together. The happiest years of my life was when I had the girls together.

I paid the mother's expenses to come up to the funeral. She arrived just as Yvonne's hearse was coming out. Michelle saw her mother and cried out, 'I want to be with my dad', and ran to me. Michelle couldn't forgive her mother. Wouldn't talk to her.

I never knew Yvonne was on drugs. If I had seen her on the drugs, I'd have taken action. She just used to drink a lager and blackcurrant when she was with me. That was all she had. She hated drink. All the young ones used to drink that Buckfast but a lager and blackcurrant was all she ever had with me. There was a home for her with me but she knew I would keep tabs on her. The crowd she hung about with, they were odd sort of friends. When she went to that rehab place in the end, she said to me, 'Dad, I want to give it up, so I'm going to try and give it up. Drugs is for mugs.' I never knew for definite till then that she had a problem with drugs.

When she was inside, she told me – 'Dad, I'm OK. I'll send you a visitor's pass'. I told her, 'Don't worry, sweetheart. When you get out, we'll have a big party for you. Your Christmas stuff will be waiting for you. Just do what you have to do', I said, 'and then come home'. The last thing she said was, 'I love you, dad'.

I was sitting having a drink, watching TV on Christmas Eve, maybe about 2 in the morning, when the police called. I thought it was one of the kids, playing Santa or having a joke. The police were at Michelle's because Yvonne used her address. They said Yvonne had died. No-one could of thought that would happen. It was totally unexpected.

I can't understand why those patrols didn't see the noose at the window when they were doing their rounds. Her room was on the ground floor. You walked right past it.

I sometimes felt she was trying to tell me something. She had some male friends too and some of them really liked her. She once said, 'It would surprise you, Dad, if I had a baby'. And she said, 'Dad, I need to have a talk with you'.

The abuse happened when she was in England. When it came out at the Inquiry that she probably had been abused, the people at work looked at me like you're a dirty old bastard. But that was put right at the Inquiry.

She liked pool. Played with me in the pub. She was very popular. She had a heart of gold. Sometimes she would come over and say, 'Sit down you two and I'll make the tea'.

When she first came up here, she contacted gay clubs right away. She used to disappear. She was in and out. She used to be looking for money. I didn't know it was for drugs. She said it was for food and things.

Inside they got no medication. When you're in prison, you need support. You shouldn't be locked up alone. I saw that cell with my lawyer. It was depressing. They should have let the girls out together, especially on Christmas Eve, to sit in the kitchen. If you talk about it, you don't get depressed. They could've locked the corridor doors and let the girls be together till 2 or 3 in the morning, then they would have gone to bed happy.

Yvonne was the kind who made her presence felt as soon as she walked into a room. I booked a club for Carolann's 21st. Yvonne walked into that club, with her hair all shaved off – her idol was that singer Sinead O'Connor – and she just drew the lassies to her. I said, 'Yer like yer faither. Yer fond of the lassies'.

She wrote to me from prison in England and told me she was gay. She said she wouldn't blame me if I didn't want to know her. I wrote back that I was sorry for her troubles about being in prison but as for the other thing, I said to her, you'll always be my wee lassie. I'll always love you. I went to see her after that – I've forgotten the name of the place. It took me all day to get there by train and I only saw her for twenty minutes. She was chuffed about the letter. She flew right into my arms.[1]

CHAPTER 2

Growing Up

CAROLANN

My mother never had any time for us. We didn't fit in with her lifestyle so she sent us off. She had a coloured child to another man and she didn't want anyone to know about us. Even when I was very young, I knew that my mother was a prostitute.

Yvonne stayed with my mother and I had to go to my aunt, my mother's sister. Michelle lived with friends of my mother. At first, the Social Services made sure we saw each other and we all went to the same primary school. When I was about ten, Michelle was sent to Nottingham for her own protection and I didn't see her for about four years.

MICHELLE

When we went back down to Leicester, I was about 8. It was only meant to be a short while that we went for to allow my dad to find some work. We stayed with my mum who I had not seen for years. She was basically a stranger. I don't think that she wanted us to stay with her. Yvonne was about four when we went down.

When we first went to Leicester I thought it was horrible and I only wanted to stay with my dad in Glasgow. My mother had a son called Leo to a black man and he stayed in the house with us. His father was not there. I think my mother was working as a prostitute at that time and she was never in the house. I was often left to look after all the younger ones when she was out and when she was home she was often drunk.

When I was about 10 years old, I was in bed one night and so were Yvonne and Leo. Carolann had moved in with my auntie because my mum couldn't handle us all. While I was lying in bed I heard screaming coming from the front of the house.

I thought it was my mum drunk again. I waited till it got quiet then I went downstairs. The house had been smashed up and the front door was kicked open. I went to the door and a neighbour came out to see if I was alright. I said I was. I went back into the house and was just going up the stairs when a woman came up the stairs behind me with a knife. She told me that if I told my mum that they were here I was getting what she was getting. She then told me to go up the stairs. I went up and checked that Yvonne and Leo were okay then I ran out the house and down the street to a friend's where I thought my mother might be. My mother was there and I told her there was someone in our house with a knife so she ran up to the house and I followed her. When I got there my mum had been stabbed in the neck. She was bleeding heavily. The police and the ambulance were called and my mum was taken to hospital.

I stayed with my aunt that night and Yvonne and Leo stayed with friends. After that I went and stayed with a friend of my mother's in Leicester but quite nearby. I stayed there for a couple of weeks. Yvonne stayed at my mum's. I stayed with those people for a while and they eventually moved to Nottingham so I went with them as my mother didn't want me. I was about 11 when I moved to Nottingham.

When I left Leicester, Yvonne was in primary school. Between the times when I first moved out the house and to moving to Nottingham I hardly ever saw Yvonne. My mother used to deny to people that Carolann and I were her daughters. In fact, my mother had a relationship with a black man called Johnny and he didn't believe we were related until Yvonne showed him the birth certificates.

After moving to Nottingham I occasionally went back to Leicester with the friends of my mum's who were looking after me and we would sometimes visit my mum's house, though I wasn't allowed to call her mum. Sometimes Yvonne would be in the house and we saw each other and we were fine. I didn't see Carolann during these visits.

CAROLANN

I was put into Social Work care and stayed with foster parents but I still saw Yvonne. She stayed at my mum's. My mum had begun a relationship with a black male called Johnny who was not the father of her son and he was indifferent towards him even if he was coloured. But Johnny and Yvonne were very friendly. When Johnny and my mum fell out, he would put her and Leo out of the house but would allow Yvonne to stay with him. I thought this was weird that it would just be him and Yvonne in the house when I used to visit them. During this time, Yvonne was quite happy and she seemed to get on well with Johnny.

Even when I got put in a children's home, I used to run away so that I could see Yvonne. Yvonne didn't go to school much and she didn't finish her secondary school. She didn't get any exams or anything. When she was about 14 or 15, she began to get into bother. She used to hang about with her pals and she would get in fights and stuff. She was a streetwise kid who was more like a boy than a girl. There was nothing feminine about her. I think she got in trouble with the police as well and eventually she was put in care. She was put in the same home as I was but I had left by then. She used to run away from the home a lot. She didn't want to be tied down and was always doing her own thing. I don't think she was into drugs at this point.[2]

SOCIAL WORKER

Ms Gilmour (Yvonne) remembers an unhappy childhood where she would be constantly assaulted by her mother. She further explains that her stepfather would witness these assaults and as a result he would be angered and, in turn, assault Ms Gilmour's mother.[3]

PSYCHIATRIST

Yvonne reports she attended Primary School and went to a few 'different Secondary Schools' because she kept being 'expelled'.[4]

SOCIAL WORKER

She remembers very little of her education and she does not recall either enjoying the experience or making friends with others within her peer group.[5]

PSYCHIATRIST

She states that she started taking drugs when she was 12 years old. She has taken 'everything.'

At 13 years, she was put into a Children's Home in Leicester. She stayed there until she was 16 years old.[6]

SOCIAL WORKER

She states that her misuse of drugs at age thirteen was due to 'hanging around with the wrong people' and initially her drug misuse involved ecstasy and cannabis. However, she quickly progressed to misusing heroin. It appears that she began to establish a pattern of shoplifting in order to finance her drug habit and then assaulting store detectives as she was apprehended.[7]

CAROLANN

When Yvonne was about 12, she had a boyfriend and she seemed quite happy for a while with him. She was just like a normal teenage girl with a boyfriend. I don't know what happened but they broke up and after that I gradually began to feel that she might be gay. I just know that she preferred girls. She told my Mum that she was gay, when she was about 15 or 16, and my Mum was sickened. For a while she didn't want to know Yvonne.

PSYCHIATRIST

Yvonne states that she has attempted suicide three times in her life. The first time was when she was 13 years old. She says this was because she was 'depressed'. 'My mum and my brother kept beating me up.' She took an overdose of all her mother's tablets. However, her mother discovered her and took her to the hospital.[8]

HOSPITAL
The Leicester Royal Infirmary

Yvonne Gilmour
The above named attended the A&E department of this hospital on 23-Feb-90.
The presenting complaint was **Overdose Paracetamol.**
Diagnosis: **Overdose Paracetamol**

The above named attended the A&E department of this hospital on 08-April-90.
The presenting complaint was **Illness.**
Diagnosis: **Drunk bruised right ankle**

The above named attended the A&E department of this hospital on 19-May-90.
The presenting complaint was **Laceration to hand.**
Diagnosis: **Left volar lac. hand**

The above named attended the A&E department of this hospital on 24-May-90.
The presenting complaint was **Assault facial injury.**
Diagnosis: **Facial laceration**

The above named attended the A&E department of this hospital on 04-Dec-90.
The presenting complaint was **Injury to left hand**
Diagnosis: **Bruised lt hand**

The above named attended the A&E department of this hospital on 22-Feb-91.
The presenting complaint was **Injury to rt ankle**
Diagnosis: **Sprain lat lig rt ankle**

The above named attended the A&E department of this hospital on 07-Oct-93.
The presenting complaint was **Fall injury to lt elbow**
Diagnosis: **Sprained ankle**[9]

PRISON CHAPLAIN

She did mention one thing that she said she hadn't told anybody before, and this was the fact that she had been sexually abused as a child That's how she started off, 'You know I have been abused. I was abused as a child'.

Did she tell you anything about the age she had been when it occurred, the sexual abuse?

No.

Did she tell you whether or not it had been a relative or not?

I don't remember.

Because, you may appreciate, Sister, that I am representing the family of Yvonne Gilmour?

Yes.

And particularly her father, and this is of course something of concern to him?

Yes.

Can you give any help to him as to any indication of when it was that this took place, because for a long time Yvonne lived down south in the custody of her mother?

Yes.

So, if you have any information that could assist the family, then I would be grateful if you could give that information?

Yes, well, I don't remember that she did say that it was a member of the family.[10]

MICHELLE

During the time I was in Nottingham, I never saw Yvonne for maybe 3 or 4 years and she didn't keep in touch. I remember that the next time I saw her was when I was pregnant and I got off the bus from work and Yvonne was waiting on me. I didn't recognise her at first as she had shaved all her hair off. She looked like a boy. I think I knew that she was gay by this time but it never bothered me. That day Yvonne only stayed for a couple of hours before she left to go to a disco. The next time I heard from Yvonne was a month after that. I was almost at the end of my pregnancy. She either phoned or wrote, I can't remember, from a prison. I don't know the name of it or where it was but I think it might've been in Essex. I'm not sure what she was in prison for but I think it could've been shoplifting and assault. I don't know if Yvonne was doing drugs at the time.

The next time I heard from her was after I had my son and I sent a letter and photograph to her at the prison. She wrote back from the prison and seemed happy for me. She told me she would come and visit on her release.

PSYCHIATRIST

Yvonne states that her second suicide attempt was when she was 16 years old and she was in Borewood Prison in Essex for assault. She tried to hang herself. She said that was sparked off because someone had stolen a knife and had hidden it in her room. She was supposed to be paroled a few days after the incident and thought that if they found the knife in her room she would lose her parole. Her last suicide attempt was a year ago in September when she was in Borewood Prison again for another assault. She was found by another inmate who saw her through the peep-hole on the door whilst trying to pass a love letter to her.[11]

CAROLANN

When I was about 18, I moved into a flat with my boyfriend and Yvonne moved in with a girl called Rosanne in the same area. She was really smitten with this girl and she was really happy. It was about this time that she came out in the gay scene and got quite involved. She really had a good time.

MICHELLE

Carolann came to visit me in Nottingham when she was pregnant. A week or so later I went to Leicester to see Carolann and Yvonne was also there. She was really good with my son and took him out for a walk. At this time she was staying with a girlfriend called Rosanne. Yvonne would be about 17 at that time. She seemed quite happy with her life.

After this meeting we all kept in touch by phoning or visiting each other. I had split up with my boyfriend and had my own flat with my son. Carolann had had her daughter by this time. Yvonne was with her when she had the baby. Yvonne stayed with Rosanne for quite a long time, maybe a couple of years, and they were both very happy. This was her first proper relationship with a girl.

Yvonne had a lot of tattoos. She had one of Rosanne on her left arm. She also has my name tattooed on her ankle with a rose and my name on it.

CAROLANN

When I was 20, my daughter was born and Yvonne was with me for the birth. But before that, she was in prison for about six months, probably for theft or assault. When she got out, I think she moved back in with Rosanne. In any case, she only lived round the corner and we saw each other a lot. She got in touch with Michelle in Nottingham and then we all kept in touch with each other and with my dad. Yvonne was in prison again for about six months, no more than a year. We didn‘t visit her there because she didn't want us to but we wrote to each other.

Yvonne told me once that she had taken an overdose in Leicester and had ended up in hospital. She didn't say why she had taken it but I think it had something to do with girlfriend problems, probably with Rosanne and her breaking up which she took quite hard. I don't think it was a serious attempt, more a cry for help. It may have been Yvonne trying to get back at Rosanne. When she was about 14, I remember, she had bad toothache and she took a lot of poppers, pain killers. She took too many and almost overdosed. I think she was taken to hospital.

Once Yvonne and I were sitting talking and she told me she had tried to hang herself. I don't remember where she was when she did it, maybe prison, but she told me that whatever she used to try and hang herself had snapped. I didn't believe what she was saying and told her not to be so stupid. I didn't think she was the sort of person to do that – she was such a strong character.

There was also the time I saw cut marks, superficial more than anything else, on her wrists a couple of years ago. The marks were not fresh and they were not too deep. I don't think Yvonne meant us to see the marks but when I did, I slapped her on the hand and said something like, 'Don't let me see something like that again or I'll slap you harder.' She didn't say anything more about it when I asked her. She didn't answer. She didn't like you to interfere in what she had done, or her life. She would shrug it off and you knew that would be it. You weren't allowed to ask her.

PSYCHIATRIST

After two and a half years Yvonne split up with her girlfriend and got her own flat. She didn't stay long in her flat, however, because she thought that perhaps her friends were using it as a 'drug den'. After leaving her flat, she came for a few weeks to Glasgow and then went to London. She was homeless there, sleeping rough. She was then put in jail for 8 months for assault. She lived with her girlfriend for a while and then the relationship broke up. She moved to Glasgow in June 1995 and stayed in a Hostel.[12]

PART TWO

Drugs and Detoxification

CHAPTER 3

Chaotic Lifestyle

MICHELLE

After a while I got my own house in Glasgow and Carolann had got her own house as well. We didn't really hear much from Yvonne, maybe the odd letter. About a year later, maybe less, she just turned up one day when I was at work. She told me she was up to stay for good though I didn't really believe her as she could never settle for long.

Yvonne stayed with me for about five months or so. She did stay for Christmas that year which I think was 1994. When she stayed with me she used to lie in her bed a lot during the day and generally laze about. She never tidied up after her and didn't help much about the house. She did start to make friends after a while and used to go to the Pollock Inn for a drink. I think she also got interested in the Glasgow gay scene as well but whenever I asked her about it she told me to mind my own business.

She began to get friendly with a well-known local drug dealer called Maggie Wattt. She actually broke into my house twice before Yvonne got involved with her. I think this was when Yvonne got herself involved in drugs. I noticed a big change in her after this and she became moody and sometimes aggressive towards me. This would be late 1994.

Early in 1995 Yvonne went back down to Leicester for a break. She said she was going to visit friends. Apparently she got in trouble during this holiday and gave a girl a beating. She was charged by the police but got out on bail. She came back to Glasgow until her court appearance. She was pretty much herself when she got back.

I think it was about spring that year that she went back to attend court. She got a prison sentence but I can't recall where she went or for how long. I moved house at that time. I got a bigger house so that Yvonne could stay with me. She wrote to me from prison, initially looking for money or clothes. I sent her a pair of trainers at one point.

POLICE CHARGE

The charge against you is that

1. on 1 June 1995 from Express store, Pollok Shopping Centre, Glasgow, you YVONNE GILMOUR did steal a quantity of jogging trousers

2. on 1 June 1995 in the concourse at Pollok Shopping Centre, Glasgow, you YVONNE GILMOUR did assault James Boyd, Security Guard and did butt him in the face and repeatedly punch him about the head to his injury.[13]

MEDICAL CORRESPONDENCE[14]

From: Brenton Medical Centre
Pollok
Glasgow

To: Drug Problem Service
Ruchill Hospital
Glasgow

Dear Sir/Madam,

re: Yvonne Gilmour dob 8.4.74
I would be grateful if this patient could be seen. She is asking for help with her drug problem. She is injecting between £60 and £80 of heroin daily.

Yours faithfully,
Dr Robertson

14 June 1995

From: Glasgow Drug Problem Service
Ruchill Hospital

To: Dr Robertson
Brenton Medical Centre

Dear Dr. Robertson,

Yvonne Gilmour – dob 08 04 74

PROBLEMS

1. IV Heroin abuse about £60 per day.
2. Temazepam oral use, three times per month, 20mgs.
3. Diazepam oral use, three times per month, approximately 20 mgs.

Thank you for sending Yvonne to the Glasgow Drug Problem Service. She has been assessed on 3 occasions. She has recently moved back to Glasgow from London and is keen for a detoxification of methadone. She tells me she had been injecting into her arms and hands and infrequently into her groin. She also attends at Pollok Addiction Service.

Yvonne has bought methadone in the past and wishes to try supervised detoxification. She has had a urine sample checked which showed benzodiazepines and morphine metabolites, it was also positive for codeine. ... Her medical showed track marks in her antecubital fossae, palpable axillary lymph nodes, normal cardiovascular system and some very interesting tattoos. She has signed our standard contract and has been prescribed methadone mixture, 40 mls, dispensed daily under supervision and diazepam 5mg x 5 daily. This diazepam dose will be reduced rapidly over the next few weeks and we will adjust her methadone as is required. She will be attending Wilson Chemists. Thank you very much for sending her to us.

Yours sincerely,
Dr Elizabeth Ross

22nd August 1995

From: Glasgow Drug Problem Service
Ruchill Hospital

To: Brenton Medical
Centre
Pollok

Dear Dr Robertson,

Yvonne Gilmour – dob 08 04 74
This woman has not attended the Glasgow Drug Problem Service since I last wrote on 28th July 1995. She has not been in contact with us and her pharmacist in Wilson Chemists has not seen her since the last week in July. I think we must regard her as lost to follow up, though wonder if she has perhaps been imprisoned. We will discharge her though we would welcome a re-referral should she re-appear.

Kind regards,
Yours sincerely,

Dr R. Sinclair
Medical Director

THE VICTORIA INFIRMARY

Discharge Report

Yvonne Gilmour Admitted 9.9.95
Discharged (irregular). 12.9.95

This young girl has just been in having developed a fever with a headache, vomiting and back pain one hour after injecting IV Heroin. There was nothing to find objectively, in particular no meningism or any sign of a septic focus. She did have a systolic murmur at the aortic area but this was short and faint and appeared inconsequential; there was certainly no stigmata of endocarditis.

On balance, therefore, I suspect this may just have been a febrile allergic reaction to some contaminant in her IV drug or maybe an intercurrent coincidental and banal viral infection.

Diagnosis at time of discharge: Heroin overdose.[15]

MICHELLE

Just before Christmas 1995, I think, Yvonne phoned my house when I was out. I called her back. She was in London, I remember. I remember shouting at her on the phone about me taking a bigger house. She sounded as if she was stoned on drugs when I called. She told me she was with friends but did not elaborate. That was the last I heard from her until just before New Year 1996. Yvonne phoned to say she wanted to come home. She was upset and crying and said she couldn't take any more. I asked her what she meant and she said that the girl she was staying with, I think her name was Terry, was taking all her money for drugs and that all she cared about was drugs. I told Yvonne to pack her stuff and come home but she said that she had no money so I told her to get on a train and that my dad would sort out the fare. She agreed to do this and I arranged for my dad to sort things out. She came up right away and moved back in with me.

She told me she wasn't well and that she couldn't sleep so I arranged for my own doctor from Pollok Health Centre to come and see her. He came out and Yvonne was obviously expecting to get DFs or something but he only gave her something to get through that day.

After that Yvonne seemed to get better and she began to help around the house. A few months after Yvonne came back to stay with me her friend Terry from London came up and she stayed for a couple of weeks. Apparently she had AIDS though at first I didn't know. I found out after Yvonne and Terry had had a fight in my dad's house. My dad phoned me to warn me what had happened. I phoned Carolann to come down in case there was trouble when Yvonne and Terry got to my house. Carolann could always handle Yvonne better than me and she came down.

Yvonne and Terry had not even got in the close when Yvonne began to get aggressive with Terry, shouting and swearing at her. I don't even know what the argument was about. Yvonne wasn't the type of person to go out of her way to cause an argument unless somebody wound her up then she would argue back. Carolann and I tried to calm Yvonne down and eventually she tried to punch me but missed. After a bit we managed to calm her down and we got her into the bedroom. She did have a drink in her. It got quiet for a while but then I heard screaming and saw that Yvonne had a knife. She began to try and cut her wrists with the knife though she didn't use too much force. I was really upset and trying to stop it because my little boy was there. Terry tried to take the knife from her but she cut her hand. I went in after Terry to the bathroom to help her but she told me she would clean her own blood up. I gathered then that she must have AIDS or something.

At this point Yvonne was still wound up and had the knife so Carolann went to get her boyfriend who was in the house nearby and she had only left a few seconds before I had to call her back because Yvonne had cornered me and Terry with the knife in her hands. It was as if she had just lost the place.

Carolann managed to get the knife off Yvonne. I then left with Carolann to go and get her boyfriend to see if he could help us. He was unable to come because he didn't have keys to lock up the house he was in. We went back over and by this time Yvonne had calmed down. She put her arms round me and began to cry, saying she was sorry. I told her if it happened again I would put her out. Terry went back to London a couple of days after that and I have heard since that she died.

After this Yvonne used to go out all day and I never really knew where she was or who she was with. All of a sudden I would go out for the day and when I came back the house would be full of Yvonne's druggie pals, usually Maggie Watt and people like her. I never actually saw her or others doing drugs in the house though I did warn her that if she did she would be finished. I knew by this time that Yvonne was injecting heroin. I used to tell her to inject out of my house and Yvonne would say, 'Would you rather that I OD'd in the house where you can find me or out in the street where you can't?' I told her that if I did catch her in the house that would be it because I didn't want the police at my door or for my son to find needles. Yvonne didn't seem to understand this though.

About this time I had another friend staying with me and Yvonne had to share a room with my son. She never used to let him into the room and I wondered if maybe she was doing drugs in the room. It worried me. After that it got from bad to worse and Yvonne got more aggressive towards me, often threatening me with violence. It got to the stage where I was not comfortable in my own house so I put her out, though I later took her back. When she came back, one day I went to look for my son's bike and found out that she had sold it. I accused Yvonne of stealing the bike and asked her how much she had sold the bike for. She told me, 'A bag.' I told her I was putting her out of the house.

CAROLANN

Yvonne phoned Michelle to say that she needed help as she was really bad on drugs and wanted us to help her. She was staying with some girls down south and one of them was HIV positive, I think she was her girlfriend, and Yvonne was scared. Yvonne came up to stay with Michelle. It was then we found out that she was injecting heroin regularly. She was heavily addicted and out of her face on drugs all the time. Her moods would change a lot and she would argue with me or Michelle a lot. Yvonne stayed with Michelle for five or six months but there was a lot of trouble. She never meant to do anything like that, it was the drugs that took over. I was the only one who could control her. My dad didn't know what was going on with Yvonne.

Yvonne stayed in hostels and moved from one to another. She seemed to sort herself out for a while but then got into bad company again and would go back on the drugs. She used to hang about with young 16 year olds who were moving into the gay scene as well. A lot of them were druggies.

I often asked Yvonne to stay with me but she always refused, I think because she knew I wouldn't put up with her carrying on. She used to bring her pals to my house and they would stay the night. She was on methadone and she also got a prescription for sleeping tablets but I think she gave the sleeping tablets away. The methadone began to make her feel depressed. She told me she wanted to come off the methadone because it made her so depressed and I think she did come off it for a while. It wasn't that she wanted to do anything to herself. It was just that she was down. It didn't help that she didn't have her own place. The hostels were getting her down. She told me that people in the hostels kept trying to get her back on the drugs and I knew that she was getting a hard time from some of the male residents at the hostel who knew she was a lesbian and would call her a 'dyke'.

CHAPTER 4

Methadone Maintenance

YVONNE'S DRUG WORKER

I first met Yvonne in 1995. At that time she was staying in the Inglefield St Hostel in Govanhill. She was referred to me for drug abuse. She was abusing heroin and Temazepam. She was interested in going on a methadone programme. I think she'd been on one before. I introduced her to Dr. Catherine Cranston's clinic and she was accepted for the methadone programme.
I was in contact with her from the summer of 1995 up until the time she died but sometimes the contact wasn't as much as others. Her methadone prescription sometimes went up and sometimes went down. But she coped for quite a while. Then she moved to the James Shields Project and it was then she started topping up.[16]

YVONNE'S GP

Can I ask you generally, Doctor, about methadone prescriptions of the sort that Yvonne was getting? Is the purpose of a prescription like that to provide a substitute for illegally obtained opiates?

That's correct.

Is it designed to stabilise what's sometimes described as a chaotic lifestyle?

Yes.

To stop, or to discourage the patient from committing crime to buy illegal drugs, for example?

That's part of the aim.

During the time that Yvonne was a patient of your practice, was she put on a drug reduction or detoxification course?

There were occasions when the doses of methadone were reduced by perhaps 5mls daily with a sort of long-term view to possibly detoxifying but that would have been very long term and, you know, in the event we decided at that time it wasn't appropriate.

So, generally speaking, it was always a methadone maintenance programme then for Yvonne, is that fair?

Yes. I don't think that was her initial aim in fact but as time went on that was what seemed most appropriate.

Do you have a lot of patients on that sort of methadone programme?

We have between, for the whole practice, for three doctors, we usually have around 20 people. We never have more than about 24 or 25 at the top limit.

Would you also have other people who might be coming off on some form of detox programme?

We occasionally prescribe a short term for detoxification, but it is relatively unusual.

Are detox programmes nowadays undertaken by places like Red Tower or do people just not go on them any more?

I think it depends very much on what the patient wants, and if patients do want to be detoxified, then it is more likely to be successful in a supervised environment like Red Tower or another rehabilitation unit, but we would occasionally undertake it in general practice in the community, if the patients want to give it a go.

As a doctor, and this may be an entirely unfair question, and if you think so just tell me. If over a period of three weeks a person was getting methadone but at reducing doses starting off at 60mls or 70mls a day and it was gradually cut down to 5mls or whatever by the end of a three week period, is that a realistic detoxification programme, in your view?

I think in the community I wouldn't do that as a realistic programme, because I think undoubtedly the person taking that course would be feeling really rough and the chances of adhering to it in the community so that at the end they were on a very small dose would be very small. I have known patients who have attempted that sort of thing in the community, and I can think of one person who managed it in his own flat. It is not outwith the bounds of possibility, but I don't think there's much doubt that the person would be feeling pretty rough.

You mentioned the number of patients on methadone programmes at your practice at any time. Are there other patients who have comparable programmes to the one that Yvonne had in terms of the length of time that they were getting methadone prescriptions and the amount that they were being prescribed from time to time?

Yes.

Would you ever stop a methadone programme like the one that Yvonne was on abruptly, in the sense of just stopping prescribing methadone altogether in one go?

I think it's unlikely that I would stop it abruptly. If the circumstances arose that I felt, for whatever reason, that I was going to stop it quickly, for example, if a patient had altered their prescription then I would consider that our doctor-patient relationship wasn't going anywhere and therefore I would be stopping the prescription, I probably would give them a reducing dose over something like a couple of weeks, knowing that it's not going to be easy for them, but rather than just stopping it abruptly and saying, don't come back.

Now it seems clear from the records that from the time Yvonne Gilmour started being prescribed methadone at your clinic in September 1995 that she continues at about the rate of 70mls. Is that quite a high level or not?

This is a moderate dose, it's slightly higher than average. The highest dose that any of my patients are on is about 120 but I know of practices where higher doses are prescribed. It is common for a dose to fluctuate to an extent. The dose is partly determined by how the patient views they are doing, and how we feel they are doing, and also by what the patient wants, because if they feel they are not getting enough methadone you are generally happy to increase it, other things being equal.

Yvonne's dose was also decreased on several occasions, in October 1995 for example.

In October Yvonne said she wished to stop methadone and her dose was reduced gradually to 40mls until January 1996. But she didn't do well and her dose was increased. It was decreased again in May because she wasn't keeping her appointments, despite warnings. I was on holiday and my partner felt that Yvonne's methadone should be reduced slightly because it's part of their side of the bargain that they do keep their appointments and don't mess us about basically.

And your part of the bargain is that you will prescribe them the appropriate dose?

Yes.

But a large part of that is an input from them as to what they need, what they feel they need?

Yes.

BY THE COURT: At the end of the day, Doctor, who controls the tap, the patient or the doctor?

The doctor.

YVONNE'S DRUG WORKER

She came to see me the middle of February, quite distressed. She had started using drugs again, on top of her prescription, and then an incident occurred at the Project with herself and another resident. She had been fighting and I think she had threatened one of the staff and had vandalised some of the building as well, and she wasn't quite sure why she had done it, and she seemed to think it was probably because she had started using again, and it was getting out of control, her urges. She got put out of the Project, so she came to see me. She was quite stressed and she asked to go and see the doctor. She said she wanted to go to Leverndale, she said that she couldn't cope with things. Maybe those weren't her exact words but that was basically what she was talking about, that she couldn't cope with what was going on, because that was her homeless again after she came out of the James Shields Project, she had basically nowhere else to go. It was her own idea to go to Leverndale and she knew it was a psychiatric hospital and when I asked her why she wanted to go there, she said she felt she needed time to sort herself out because things were getting on top of her. And there were other things upsetting her like her close friend having died.

I took her to Dr Cranston who saw her and gave her a referral for Leverndale.

YVONNE'S GP

What happened was that on the 20th February 1996, Yvonne's drug worker phoned up and said that Yvonne had come to see her and she was very concerned about her, and we agreed that she should bring her to the surgery, and then I saw her. Her mood was very low, and in fact she seemed to me to be a bit withdrawn, in that she obviously was far from her normal self, and rather than sort of pouring out her problems she was very much sort of withdrawn and into herself, and on specific questioning, even when you asked specific questions, she didn't seem able to, she wasn't very good at answering them, and we asked things like, you know, what did she see about the future and she just couldn't contemplate it, but it was actually quite difficult to get much out of her that day. Normally, when she was attending the clinic, if she was having problems she was usually quite up front about it. I can't remember what she said specifically about suicidal ideation, I did mention it, but I remember I was concerned about her and I would have regarded her trying to commit suicide as a possibility, if we hadn't taken further action. That was one of my concerns. The referral to Leverndale was certainly partly prompted by this concern because her mood was very low and she clearly wasn't her normal self. In the referral letter – I don't have a copy of it – but the gist of it would have been that Yvonne had a drug problem, that she was on our methadone programme, but the letter would have made clear that that was not the reason for referral. My reason for referral was that I was concerned about the fact that she seemed quite depressed and I felt because of that she needed further assessment.

MICHELLE

One day after I hadn't seen Yvonne for a while, maybe about February, she turned up at my work at Leverndale Hospital. Another girl I was talking to suddenly said, 'Look, there's your sister' and I thought she was just up to visit me for something and then she said she was up to get admitted. Well, at that point she wasn't sure if she was getting admitted or not. She was with her drugs counsellor. I didn't ask her about it because people are in Leverndale for all sorts, depression, drugs, drink, suicide, things like that. I mean, it is a mental hospital anyway. It turned out she was only in for a week or so. She went to ward 4 which is for addicts, alcoholics and people suffering from depression. Because Yvonne was my sister, I wasn't allowed to work in the same bit that she was admitted to, so I got moved to another bit of the hospital.

YVONNE'S DISCHARGE SUMMARY FROM LEVERNDALE HOSPITAL

Admitted: 20.02.96 Discharged: 27.02.96
Diagnosis: **Opiate Dependent Syndrome**

1. Referred by her GP and accompanied by her Social Worker/ Drug Worker. Her presenting complaint was depression.
2. Over the last week she described herself as being depressed. She states that she has had difficulty in getting to sleep and going to sleep at 3.00a.m. and wakening up at 7.00a.m. or 8.00a.m. She said she had no appetite and has not been drinking. She doesn't know, however, if she is losing weight. She describes her concentration as being poor and her mood

> as being very low. In fact, she says she has been contemplating suicide over the past few days. She said, 'I was going to jump in the Clyde'.
>
> When asked about the future, she said, 'I don't plan the future, I just live day to day. Ever since I was a little girl, everything has gone wrong. I don't have much of an opinion of myself.'

She was a rather ill-kept young lady with a nose ring. She was rather glum, but was easy to make contact with. She had no noticeable mannerisms. Her behaviour was appropriate. Her mood was rather flat. Stream of thought – this was rather reluctant, slow and she mumbled a lot. Thought-content – she had no obsessional thoughts or compulsions. There were no ideas of reference. She did not have any delusions but reports that she has had visual and auditory hallucinations while on drugs and whilst withdrawing from drugs. Her intelligence was below average. Her memory was good. Her attention and concentration were poor. Her insight was also good.

This lady clearly has an opiate dependent syndrome. She was admitted because of depressive symptoms and possible suicidal ideas. Whilst on the ward, she was sociable and showed no signs whatsoever of depression or any suicidal intent.

Whilst an in-patient the patient remained rather difficult with staff, showing a consistently belligerent attitude. There was no evidence of any depressive illness during her admission and she appeared to socialise with a small group of patients, playing music loudly in the Day Room. On two occasions during her admission other patients reported that they had been offered drugs by Yvonne. Although she was only confronted on one occasion she denied this. However, we are inclined to be suspicious that she was taking extra medication while in hospital.

The patient was referred to the Community Drug Project at the Southern General Hospital. This would allow any further monitoring of her mental state and any necessary psychiatric treatment be instigated. Her appointment was for one week after discharge but unfortunately she did not attend. No further arrangements will be made.

YVONNE'S GP

After her discharge from Leverndale, Yvonne continued to attend the clinic and remained on the same methadone maintenance dose of 50mls, until 14th March. She came to the clinic that day and after the clinic the patients that I haven't seen we discuss with the drug workers and on that occasion I was told that Yvonne herself felt that 50mls wasn't enough and requested an increase in dose, which we agreed to. Yvonne's dose was increased to 60mls and she attended the clinic regularly. On one occasion in the middle of April she did not show up but we had a message that she was held up at court.

When Yvonne attended the surgery she was not necessarily seen by myself although it was usually myself who wrote the prescription. On some occasions she would be seen only by the drug counsellors, who do a clinic at our surgery, and we see any patient that there is any concern about. On one particular day, 25th April 1996, she attended and saw the drug counsellors as normal but she also made an appointment to see myself and in my notes I've written 'Cousin had accuphase injection and Naltrexone' which is a kind of treatment, which in fact Yvonne was telling me about, for a quick kind of opiate withdrawal. Yvonne was asking that I would refer her to Dr Baird, who is based at Leverndale and has a clinic at the Victoria Infirmary, with a view to her also having this treatment, the reason being that she was expecting a sentence. She was expecting to be in the prison for a period and didn't want to be withdrawing from drugs during that period. Accuphase is basically a major tranquilliser, but it is long-acting, and can be given by injection. Up until then, I had only heard rumours about this treatment.

MEDICAL CORRESPONDENCE[17]

From: Dr Cranston. To: Dr Baird, Victoria Infirmary

GP's Letter 26 04 96

Dear Dr Baird,

This 22 year old girl has specifically requested referral to yourself for consideration of detoxification from Methadone.
I understand her cousin (Alice Mills) was treated with Accuphase and Naltrexone under your care. Yvonne thinks her cousin may have mentioned about her to yourself.

At any rate, Yvonne joined our practice when she was living at the hostel at 218 Bath St. She started using heroin over 2 years ago now. She was started on the Methadone programme in September 1995 and has been relatively stable on this. She is currently on 60ml daily (supervised dispensing), as well as 2 Chloral hydrate capsule at night. She has also used Temazepam, although my impression is that she has not been doing so recently, at least, not heavily.

I am not sure about Yvonne's motivation to remain drug free long-term. She is honest enough to say that part of her reason for wanting to come off Methadone at present is because there is a likelihood of her getting a prison sentence.

I should also mention that she had an admission to Leverndale in February of this year. At that time, she was feeling very depressed and was, possibly, suicidal. However, her main problem is thought to be opiate dependence, rather than a depressive illness.

Thank you for seeing Yvonne,
Yours sincerely

Dr Cranston

From: Dr Baird
Consultant Psychiatrist
Leverndale Hospital

To: Yvonne Gilmour

15 May 1996

Dear Ms Gilmour

We have received a referral letter from your GP, Dr Cranston, referring you to the psychiatric services and specifically to Dr Baird.

Dr Baird is going on holiday imminently but has asked me to write to you to say that he will make arrangements to see you preliminary at his offices here in Leverndale Hospital upon his return in early June.

Yours sincerely
Dr Baird's Secretary

YVONNE'S GP

I don't know if Yvonne ever saw Dr Baird. I don't know if she received an appointment or not, but I certainly wasn't aware of a meeting.[18]

CHAPTER 5

Hostel Living

BLUE TRIANGLE HOSTEL, ASSISTANT MANAGER

Blue Triangle hostel is a hostel project which provides 24 hour supported accommodation for up to 32 young homeless persons, both male and female, between the ages of 18 and 25. The primary aim is to prepare residents for independence within the community. There are a myriad of problems ranging from mental health, drugs, homelessness and both physical and mental abuse. A care plan is drawn up for each resident and assistance is given with finance budgeting, health issues, social skills, education, etc. Each resident is assigned a key worker.

Yvonne came to us at the end of February from Leverndale through her drug worker. It was very difficult for us to work with Yvonne the first couple of months that she moved into Inverlochy Street because she simply wasn't there on a regular basis for you to build up a good support plan, but when she was she was still paying her heating and lighting charges.
She looked happy enough. She looked like she was in control of perhaps the amount of medication that she was being prescribed by her GP and I think maybe after three months there was a decline. Looking through the records you can see that quite clearly.[19]

Extracts from Records

20th March 1996

Yvonne says she's settled in OK. She finds it difficult on occasions when remarks are made by other residents about her sexuality and drug abuse. She's aware of the importance of keeping her appointments with her doctor if she wants to keep her methadone script. She complains that the amount of methadone she's on is not enough but she appears to be coping and not topping up. She said the breakdown which led her to hospital was caused by the death of her partner. Apparently, she woke up one morning to find her dead in the bed beside her. She is still feeling the effects of this and has not really grieved and feels that this contributed to her nervous breakdown and resultant eviction from her last hostel.

She feels quite isolated in this area. I offered to get numbers of Lesbian and Gay groups for her.

She has outstanding court charges which I'll try to clarify with her lawyer.

24th April 1996

Yvonne does not use the hostel very often, comes in once a week to collect Giro then goes. I spoke to her briefly yesterday, says she's OK and staying with a friend. She is in five weeks rent arrears and should be issued a first warning for this.

31st April 1996

Has been around a bit more at the week-end. Had arranged to see her on Sunday but she had a phone call from her partner early on to say that a relative had died so she left to give her support. Need to speak to her about her rent and outstanding charges (which she's aware of). There's a lot of work to be done with Yvonne. If she were only around more often we could get started.

10th June 1996

Yvonne had a relapse last Tuesday, used heroin and used all her money. She plans to get money from her father which will get her through until next payment is due. She is very depressed. She did not go for her methadone script again today. We spoke at some length tonight about how much support she needs and where to get it. She sees her drug worker on a Thursday at the doctor's surgery. I suggested looking for a drugs project. Her relationship has ended which is adding to her depression – she does not have any contacts within the gay community which she feels would support her. I went through various ones with her again and she said she would think about it. She wants to work out a budgeting plan with me and to be taken shopping next Tuesday. Admits she does not handle her money well. The detox at Leverndale seems to be getting arranged by her ex-partner. It all sounds rather vague and I wonder whether it will happen as quickly as she says. There are a lot of problems to be worked on. Says she will be around more now that she has split with her partner. Seven weeks rent arrears.

19th June 1996

Yvonne was arrested last week on outstanding charges: Was given 250 pounds fine to be paid at 3 pounds per week. She also spent five days without her methadone which affected her badly. Yesterday she looked rough, she said this was because she'd not had her script. I had some doubts about this. I went with her to see her bail officer at Sheriff Court. She will see the bail officer 2-3 times per week. Appointments will be made weekly and if for any reason Yvonne can't make it she must phone them, otherwise she could be arrested. They will also come to see her here. The interim diet is on 5th August, trial on 26th August 10a.m. Sheriff Court. Will have to do a court report for her. If Yvonne co-operates with bail officer it would be in her favour. No word of the detox happening yet. Bus tickets have been supplied to enable her to keep appointments with bail officer. I'm concerned about Yvonne's emotional state right now – her break up with her partner is hurting her badly. She needs time to talk whenever she needs to.

10 July 1996

Outstanding warrants out for Yvonne, two assaults and two vandalism and one breach of peace. Contacted lawyer who will be phoning back today. Yvonne is very anxious about this, frightened of cold turkey if she gets a sentence. She'd been doing well this week, doing the lawns and in general appeared to be stable. She spent a lot of time in the office talking to staff.

Phoned bail officer to explain what was happening and that she may not be able to keep her appointment as we are waiting for the lawyer's advice.

17th July 1996

Yvonne has been staying at her partner's since last Wednesday. There's a warrant out for her arrest. Plan was to hand herself in today and appear at District Court. Will know later today what the result is.

YVONNE'S GP

Yvonne came to the practice with her key worker from the hostel the day after her release from Cornton Vale (where she had been in custody from 17th July till 31st July) and was very insistent about wanting to go back on methadone. I considered this appropriate. We knew she had a history of IV drug abuse. She had quite an unsettled lifestyle and when we had been prescribing methadone to her she did seem to get certain benefits from that. She had said at the very beginning that her long-term aim was to be drug free but she didn't see it in the foreseeable future. And for someone that had a drug problem just coming out of custody and living in a hostel I think it would be unrealistic to expect them to remain drug free.

When people come out of custody, we have to start them on a lower dose because we assume they've lost their tolerance to opiates. If we did not prescribe methadone for them coming out of custody, I think the likelihood is that they would be feeling dreadful and start using street drugs. The particular risk there is that they will have lost some of their tolerance to opiates but they will go and buy whatever they would usually buy and overdose. That's quite a recognised thing. We started Yvonne on 40mls but she was soon struggling and she had either been using illicit drugs or feeling very strongly tempted to use illicit drugs, so we agreed to increase her dose to 50mls in August.

1st August 1996

Yvonne had an Intermediate Pleading Diet at Sheriff Court on 5/8/96. Her bail was continued unsupervised. She appears again at District Court Tuesday 13/8/96. She intends to plead guilty and do the sentence which should be 30 days. She prefers to get it out of the way rather than have a fine or probation. I've found her a bit hyper this week – very excitable and aggressive verbally at times. Still experiencing a lot of hurt over her break up with her partner. I'm concerned that she may start using again. She says things like there's no point in trying to stay off. Her self-esteem is very low right now and the pressure of these court cases is affecting her badly. She's to make an appointment with the lawyer this week to discuss trial on the 26th. I'll try to go with her.

14th August1996

Formal Written Warning

Paraphernalia for using drugs found in her room – destruction of hostel property (i.e.burnt knives and spoons) – offensive weapon (chair leg) found in room.

Counselled to maintain regular contact with drug worker and regular urine analysis.

21st August 1996

Yvonne did not keep doctor's appointment on Monday. Said she'd no bus fares. She'd had a drink on Monday night and I spoke to her about this when on shift. She also said she wasn't well enough to go to see her lawyer and cancelled the appointment. She rearranged this for Thursday 4p.m. Spoke to Yvonne's drug worker about my concern that if Yvonne does not have her script she must be taking something else. Yvonne is unwell again today and not planning to keep her doctor's appointment today.

25th September 1996

Met with Yvonne yesterday. I felt strongly that Yvonne was out of control in several areas, her drug taking, alcohol intake, her emotional state. Using any means to block out what's going on in her life. I'd spoken to her last week re Hepatitis C counselling – she hadn't responded to any of my suggestions and her behaviour was a cause for concern. I felt her place here was in jeopardy if these issues were not addressed. I listed all my concerns and we discussed conditions of stay for the future (it was a very frank discussion). Yvonne has now gone to register at Easterhouse Health Centre and also gone to Easterhouse Drugs Initiative and must go on a regular basis and actively seek help through counselling. She says she's been using daily and shoplifting to supply the money. She has several more charges coming up and I've suggested that she sees her lawyer ASAP to clarify exactly what is coming up when. I have doubts whether Yvonne can sustain being drug free and also suggested she consider rehab. She has a lot of issues to tackle. Her conditions of stay have been made very clear to her. 10 weeks rent arrears.

2nd October 1996

Review of Placement

Initially Yvonne appeared to be doing well in the hostel, she maintained her methadone script, paid rent and budgeted well for herself. After a period in Cornton Vale prison, she admitted to topping up and did not take up on offers to arrange counselling or rehab before crisis point was reached. Yvonne seemed to be of the opinion that the occasional hit was OK. In reality she was spending 20 pounds daily and shoplifting to supply her habit.

Aims and Objectives Achieved:

Some measure of stability in the first few months. Lost motivation to be drug free.

Aims and Objectives Not Achieved:

The sustaining of her methadone script without topping up. Actively seeking help through counselling or rehab.

Eviction Report

2nd October 1996

Evicted due to continuous relapses and use of heroin.
If she is successful in stabilising on a methadone script, we will reconsider her.
Resident refused to sign.

HOSTEL ASSISTANT MANAGER

And during your involvement with Yvonne Gilmour did you form any impression as to whether she could be described as being suicidal at any time?

I wouldn't describe her as suicidal.

Would headstrong be a fair description?

Oh, yes, she was, very headstrong.

Yvonne was a self-confessed shoplifter which she did only to feed her drug habit. When she came to the hostel initially she didn't have the same need to go shoplifting as she wasn't abusing drugs over and above her script to begin with and she appeared to be getting on with her life in general. She was, in fact, an ideal resident ... and she appeared to be generally, fairly happy. After a month or so she started having problems, I think resulting from the failure of a relationship and when the relationship deteriorated, so did Yvonne's standard of life. She consequently returned to drug abuse.

She was having terrible problems with drugs. I remember she expressed very grave doubts about being incarcerated in Cornton Vale without getting her methadone and she was certainly having sleepless nights here at the hostel thinking about it. She realised that since she had come here she was able to see a good progression in herself and that she was handling life a lot better even although she took a backwards step when the relationship with her girlfriend deteriorated.

I think she believed that given the chance to stay here, she would have been able to get herself back on the rails again – as long as she was getting the methadone to keep things under control. As I say, the thought of going to a custodial sentence at Cornton Vale really frightened her.

While she was waiting on her trial I remember she became very excitable and aggressive and verbally abusive towards everyone.

Due to Yvonne's lack of commitment to the programme, she was eventually asked to leave. This was due to her continued relapse and use of heroin which we cannot at all condone in the project. We took into account that Yvonne was receiving a lot of support from the project itself, from her key worker, from her drugs worker and from the Easterhouse Drugs Initiative. However, nothing appeared to be helping and despite her earlier promise she appeared to be going vastly downhill and back to her old ways.

I personally would think that Yvonne would find it almost impossible to survive in Cornton Vale without her methadone script and the assistance of a drugs counsellor.

CAROLANN

When she last got out of prison, she told me she wanted off the drugs and wanted to go to a detox centre. I told her to do it for herself and not for others. She seemed really keen to get off the drugs. I think she might have been trying because I never saw her stoned at the this time. She got tired quite a lot, probably because she was coming off the drugs. Her drug counsellor was trying to help Yvonne and was trying to get her a flat. She said Yvonne would get her own flat when she was clean and Yvonne seemed to be looking forward to that. Michelle and I said we would help her out when she got her own flat and Yvonne seemed keen to take my girls for visits when she got her flat.

CHAPTER 6

Detox Centre

YVONNE'S GP

Yvonne didn't attend the clinic on release from Cornton Vale (where she was in custody from 3rd September till 17th September). She came about a month later, on the 14th October. She had been uisng heroin, about two and a half grammes a day intravenously, and she had also been taking Temazepam, 10 to 15 a day by mouth. It's very difficult to say how that equivalates to 50mls of methadone because when you buy heroin on the street, you don't know how much is heroin and how much is anything else, but that amount is roughly the same as she was taking when she came to our practice in the beginning.

There was mention of Yvonne going to the Red Tower drug rehabilitation in Helensburgh. We weren't directly involved in organising this but we were very happy about it. This was an indication that Yvonne was taking it upon herself to try and tackle her drug problem. She told me that she was hoping to go from Red Tower into a long-term rehabilitation unit. She was talking about Malta House in Edinburgh. I felt at the time Yvonne was fairly positive about things and also quite realistic about things. The reason she came to see me on the 14th was because this admission to Red Tower was planned and she wanted to be on methadone up until her admission, and we discussed things and agreed that that would be appropriate, but she did seem quite positive about the thing. I think she certainly had been abusing drugs, abusing illegal drugs, how heavily I couldn't comment, but I mean there are certain times in our records that, you know, she admitted to us that she had been using drugs and said that she was struggling on her prescription. But I would have said that rehabilitation would have been a good thing for Yvonne, I think that when people with drug problems come to the stage that they would consider rehabilitation then it is a step in the right direction, and I think, particularly with someone like Yvonne who has maybe had quite a difficult background and doesn't have the benefit of a stable environment to address the problems, then a rehabilitation unit can sometimes offer them that. But her motivation, I think, was because she expected to be going to prison rather than the fact that she thought she would be able to come off drugs and stay off them completely. The motivation was because she was likely to be in a position where she couldn't get drugs.

I would have considered Yvonne at risk but I wouldn't at that time have considered her at any more risk than any other drug users I know. By at risk, I mean at risk of coming to harm from her drug use, as in medical problems or overdose, you know, inadvertent overdose.

CAROLANN

About October Yvonne went to a drugs rehabilitation centre in Helensburgh called Red Tower. We weren't allowed to see her there because the staff thought we might take drugs to her which wouldn't have been the case. After a couple of weeks there, Yvonne phoned me once a week. She sounded a lot better than when she'd gone in. She seemed quite happy and said a girl she knew had packed up and left. Yvonne said she could do the same if she wanted but she wanted to stick it out. She did say it was hard but that she wanted to do it for us. I told her again to do it for herself so that at least once in her life she could do something for herself and not other people.

Red Tower[20]

The Red Tower Drugs Project in Helensburgh is run by the Catholic Church and is funded by contributions from Greater Glasgow Health Board and from Local Authority Social Work Departments. It is a residential centre for young people who are tackling drug problems.

Extracts from Contract of Admission

1. DRUGS/ALCOHOL ABUSE
Anyone suspected of drug/alcohol misuse (including misuse of prescribed medication) will be discharged. You will be asked to provide urine samples for analysis on a routine basis.

2. VISITORS
Family visits are not allowed unless a child access visit is being arranged.

3. REMAINING IN BUILDING
Residents are not permitted to leave the building unless a staff member is present with them. Failure to comply may result in discharge.

4. PARTICIPATION
Residents are expected to take part fully in all activities.

8. PHYSICAL ABUSE
Any form of physical abuse towards residents/staff will result in discharge and possible prosecution.

9. BULLYING AND INTIMIDATION
Any complaints of bullying or intimidation will be investigated and will result in discharge if allegations are substantiated.

11. RELATIONSHIPS
Relationships of an intimate nature are strongly discouraged in Red Tower because it can hamper personal progress. Failure to co-operate may result in discharge.

13. No parcels will be accepted. They will be returned to sender. There are no exceptions to this rule.

PROJECT MANAGER

BY THE COURT: Would it be fair to say that there was a certain element of truth perhaps in Miss Gilmour's description of Red Tower as being worse than prison?

One would hope not, my Lord, but I understand that clients coming in may find it difficult to understand that if we are going to assist them we need a fairly controlled and measured environment.

Yes, I mean, what is the environment? I mean, is it dormitories, or single rooms?

The building is a large red sandstone building. We have a number of single rooms, a number of double rooms and two three-bedroomed rooms.

Sounds a bit like Cornton Vale so far, yes. Yes, what else?

We have a large lounge, a reception area, dining room. We have medication room, we have offices for staff and they have a recreation room which has a table tennis in it, television and so on.

Now, they don't go out of the building. I mean, they may go out of the building, but they don't go out of the grounds, is that correct, unless they are going to a specific...?

No, unless they are going with a member of staff we would ask them to remain within the building. Obviously, in better weather we use the grounds as well.

Yes?

Because we have a quarter of an acre of ground.

Yes. And what's your total complement of clients?

We have 23 beds in all.

And I mean, what is the regime? I mean, is it up and doing gym in the morning, or is it sitting about thinking about things, or a mixture or what?

Initially when clients come in we give them a period of settling in, usually it's a period of approximately a week, but unless someone was medically unfit they would have to take part in all activities every day, which is up in the morning, breakfast is an optional, but after breakfast we have a long meeting.

Uh huh?

They do some light exercises, we discuss the plans for the day, we'll have a meditation class. Although we have full domestic staff, clients have the responsibility for chores in the house.

Yes?

They will carry these out, we will administer medication and then we have structured group work twice during the day and clients will come together hopefully in groups of five or six or seven to work on, it could be coping with your emotions, it could be assertiveness training, it could be improving your physical health. We also take part in a number of recreational activities using the local swimming pool during the day and occasionally we have support from specialist outdoor resource centres for sailing, or something like that, and we provide all those, and we have, the residents also have meetings of their own when they can raise issues which they would like us to look at.

Am I right in thinking that although it is run by the Archdiocese of Glasgow it's not a particularly catholic or indeed christian set up?

No, the organisation accepts applications from clients of all faiths and employs staff of all faiths as well. I would say we have a broadly christian, with a small 'c', ethos, a humanitarian ethos, but there is no specific religious component.

It was just you talked about meditation, and I was wondering what exactly you meant by that?

Well, the meditation might be based upon a christian act, or it may be based upon an article from a humanistic thought, but it would be a meditation asking people to focus on a thing, like, let's all focus on being more considerate to another person today, looking at your own feelings. You know, explore how angry you were yesterday, something like that.

How do you measure success?

We do not have a tool for measuring success. I would say our measure of success is that at least for a short period at a time people are in a safer environment than out on the street using drugs.

Now, you've told us that your aim was detoxification not rehabilitation, so essentially then are you just drying people out in

the hope that once they are dried out, although they are going back to the same milieu as that from which they came they will not in fact go back into the drug scene?

Our hope would be, our hope is slightly broader than that, it would be that whilst detoxifying, along with the person who had referred them to the project who has ongoing care and management we would be able to facilitate longer term rehabilitation through one of our other agencies. The Church of Scotland have a number of long term projects and we have a good working relationship with these groups. We would hope, earnestly hope that the clients would not return to the environment after a short period of time

When Yvonne Gilmour was admitted on 1st November 1996, she was prescribed a methadone mixture, which is an opiate substitute, along with a course of Diazepam, which is an anti-anxiolytic drug. The original methadone prescription was 60 mls and we would reduce weekly by 10mls a week. Shortly after admission she complained of low mood and was prescribed Prothiaden which is an anti-depressant medication. Feelings of low mood are not particularly unusual and during her time on the project Yvonne did talk about a grief reaction to the death of a former partner. She continued this medication in reducing doses for some time and then, as is quite often the case, she transferred to another reducing scale using morphine sulphate and Diazepam. This allows someone to reduce their medication more quickly than using methadone. Yvonne would have finished this course about the 2nd December but she was discharged from the project on 28th November.

Why was Yvonne discharged on 28th November?

Yvonne had had a number of difficulties in the project and had received counselling and various warnings, but the events accumulated and the night before there was an incident where another resident was struck in the face. There were no independent witnesses, but from our interviews and discussions with people it appears that Yvonne had struck another woman in the face, causing her tooth to protrude through the flesh of the cheek. This was discussed with her and it was felt that the only safe, reasonable course of action was to ask her to leave.

Even although she was almost at the end of her detoxification?

That's correct.

How did Yvonne react to the news on 28th November that she was being discharged that very day?

She was very distressed, tearful, explaining that she had nowhere to go and she was very distraught by the whole event. She became particularly agitated when asked to go to her room to pack her things and threatened to jump off the first floor balcony and she had to be physically restrained. She also broke a picture frame and grabbed a piece of the glass threatening to cut herself. She was very distressed.

Did you witness this?

No, it was reported by the care officer who was with her.

On the 15th of November, it would appear from the records that Yvonne was picked up from Red Tower for escort to the Court in Glasgow. She was informed that she was due to attend Glasgow Sheriff Court but when she got there was informed it must have been the District Court. On attending the District Court Yvonne stated that her solicitor did not appear and her case was put back.

Yes, that is correct.

Now, because she had been out of the centre on the 15th of November, did she then have to go through some further testing?

It would be normal to obtain a urine analysis on return from the Court.

And that was to make sure that while they had been out of the centre the client had not had access to any other...?

Yes.

Any other drugs other than the ones prescribed?

That's correct.

And do the results show that she did not have any access to any other drugs, other than what she was prescribed

Yes. We were happy with the result.

The next day, Yvonne appeared to have been annoyed at having to produce a urine sample. I quote from the records: *Yvonne greatly annoyed this morning by having to produce urine sample owing to court yesterday. Informed that this was standard procedure and she was no different from other residents who have been out of the project*

Yes.

Now, in the afternoon section it states *Yvonne came to staff complaining that she had been struck by a male resident. Apparently Yvonne had been involved in a verbal exchange with another female resident and the male resident had intervened striking her on the body and in the face. Staff investigated and received independent confirmation from two residents that Yvonne had not provoked this action.*

Yes.

CAROLANN

The second time Yvonne phoned from the rehab place she told me you could get in trouble there if you got in a fight. She said she had taken a kicking from a boy there who was a patient. She said she just lay there and took the beating because she didn't want to get put out. She had a black eye and bruising to her legs. I think the boy that did it got put out.

PROJECT MANAGER

So this is one of the issues that you were talking about when you said there had been some difficulty with Yvonne at the centre?

Yes, Yvonne had a number of difficulties in terms of relating to other people in the project.

Yes?

She didn't feel comfortable with group living. She wasn't comfortable with staff, she found authority quite challenging and she was quite assertive about her sexuality and at the same time she appeared to be, I don't know what the correct way to put it is, but she appeared to have a chip on her shoulder, so she there were two sides to the coin as far as her sexuality was concerned. She was very open about it but she would also see anyone's comments in general directed at her.

So the background to the verbal exchange had been something to do with Yvonne's sexuality?

Yes, that's correct.

And as you say, on the one hand she was assertive about it?

Yes.

She would be open about it?

Yes.

But did you also get the impression that she was sensitive about it?

Yes, a number of times it is recorded in the notes that she came saying that people were talking about her and were actually talking to her and being derogatory and offensive to her about her sexuality.

Yvonne was spoken to by her key worker and issued a warning for her general attitude towards residents and staff.

Yvonne explained that she had been receiving a great deal of verbal abuse from residents mainly over her sexuality. However she did agree that her manner was often too extreme. She stated that she would try and tone down her manner and look at herself in this respect.

Yes.

***And she was also told that she would be spoken to regarding incident.* What does that mean?**

It meant that the key worker spoke to her and probably that would be followed up by a member of the management team reiterating that this was important and she would have wanted her to work on it.

And could we look at the 17th of November and does it say there *Yvonne's mood is much more settled today. Feels she is making a huge effort in controlling her temper.*?

Yes, that's correct.

So it would appear that she had taken on board what had been said the day before?

It would appear so.

Now if you could turn to the 21st of November please?

Yes.

Does it say there *Spent some time with Yvonne this morning as she was finding it difficult to come to terms with the death of a previous partner.*

Yes, that is correct.

Now was it the case in your centre that when your clients were going through the reducing regime, a detoxification process, that they would want to discuss with you issues that were coming to the fore when they were withdrawing?

Yes, that is correct

And in Yvonne's case was one of the things that was upsetting her this previous bereavement that she had had?

She certainly voiced that on this occasion and I believe on a number of occasions..

Now the next entry I would like you to look at is the 23rd of November.

Yes.

And does it say there *Yvonne emotional this morning, had an outburst with two members of staff, wanting to leave, but asked by staff to go to her room and calm down. This she did and apologised to the staff and did not want to self-discharge?*

Yes, that is correct.

By this time she had been in the centre since the 1st of November, and this is now the 23rd?

Yes, that's correct.

In your experience did there come a point when the client found it difficult to cope?

Yes, there are a number of points we would expect to see clients anxious to leave. After perhaps four or five days and then perhaps after four weeks, there appear to be all those thresholds where the person feels that they can no longer stay, so it would not be unusual for a client to express such emotions at approximately this time.

Now can you please turn to the entry for the 27th of November?

Yes.

And does it say there *On hearing a loud discussion coming from Yvonne's room a member of staff entered at 7p.m. to find another female resident bleeding profusely. After situation was diffused Yvonne stated that she was acting in self-defence.*

That is correct.

As far as you are concerned was the aspect that she was acting in self-defence investigated?

Yes.

And were the police called in?

No, we don't ordinarily involve the police. It would be most unusual for us to involve the police unless, of course, a client had indicated that they wished to press charges. Our clients perhaps don't have quite a good relationship with the police and it is sometimes counter-productive to involve them.

When Yvonne was interviewed, did she maintain that she had been acting in self-defence?

To my recollection we interviewed Yvonne, we interviewed the resident who had been assaulted and I do not recall Yvonne reiterating the act of self-defence. My best recollection is she discussed that this other person had been speaking ill of her.

So, in fact, what she was saying was that she was being provoked?

Yes, that would be my recollection of it.

RED TOWER CARE OFFICER

Following discussion with management Yvonne was discharged from Red Tower. She was very upset and I was asked to sit with her. Shortly after entering the room, both Yvonne and another member of staff present, Yvonne attempted to leave room via balcony. Stated she was going to jump. Yvonne had to be stopped from doing so and I managed along with the other staff member to get her to the bed. At this point the assistant manager came into the room. Yvonne was very emotional and upset and with her foot smashed a glass-framed photograph on her bedroom floor. She then picked up a piece of glass. She refused to let go of this and again I had to restrain her to prevent any harm. The assistant manager then spoke to her and she gave him the piece of glass. Yvonne then became calmer and I remained with her until she did so. She made a call to her partner re being discharged and arrangements are being made for the possibility of her drug worker picking her up from the project. This was not possible and Yvonne had to leave by train. Her belongings were left at Red Tower to be arranged to be brought to her tomorrow. Yvonne left at 3.25p.m. on a train to Glasgow. It was arranged that Yvonne would call Project to enquire about possible medication from her GP. Yvonne's GP was not available but I spoke to another doctor at her practice who agreed to provide medication for her.

PROJECT MANAGER

When would Yvonne have left the project if she had completed the course that was outlined for her?

The normal duration would have been about eight weeks. If it was felt appropriate that she should stay longer, then her drugs worker would apply for funding, we can't keep someone without money coming from an external source but the normal duration is in fact about eight weeks. We would hope that by about the six week stage arrangements for after care would be made with another project. The main focus of our work is detoxification, not rehabilitation.

Did you secure Yvonne a place in any project at the time of her discharge?

We did secure an agreement that the YMCA in Renfrew would offer her accommodation.

The YMCA is not a rehabilitation centre?

No, it is purely accommodation.

CHAPTER 7

Arrest

YVONNE'S GP

On the 28th November we received a telephone message at the practice from one of the drug workers to say that Yvonne had been thrown out of Red Tower but that he wanted us to prescribe short term for her as a detoxification regime. My colleague spoke to Red Tower and then prescribed Yvonne 30 milligrams MST, which is long-acting morphine tablets, on a nine-day course. She was given three tablets twice daily for three days, two tablets twice daily for three days and then one tablet twice daily for three days. It was my partner who dealt with this but it is unusual for us to prescribe these morphine tablets and the fact that he was asked specifically to prescribe those would make me think that that was what she was getting while she was in Red Tower. Shortly after that Yvonne's records were requested by another practice in Renfrew where she had registered on the 4th December.[21]

CAROLANN

The next thing was that Yvonne turned up at Michelle's with a girlfriend called Linda, Linda McGill. She and Yvonne were staying at a hostel in Renfrew. I don't know how she ended up there. She told us that her time in the rehab was up but my dad phoned up later and found out that she had been put out for fighting. Yvonne seemed fine, laughing and joking and taking the mickey out of me and Michelle. She didn't say if she was on drugs or not but I asked her if she was still on them and she said it was hard. She said she still had a craving for it. Linda said they were both looking out for each other to keep off drugs. I didn't think Yvonne would go back to jagging heroin but thought that she might go back to taking jellies. She had a

T-shirt on and I saw that there were no fresh marks on her arm. I asked her if she and Linda were girlfriends and she said yes.

Yvonne stayed the night at Michelle's with Linda. I also stayed there that night and we had a good laugh. The next morning Michelle went to work and Yvonne and Linda left before 10 o'clock. She told me she was going to the Social in Paisley for a claim. I don't think she had any money.

MICHELLE

Yvonne was about four weeks into the programme at Red Tower when the police came to my door asking for her. They told me they had a warrant for her arrest for non-appearance at court and this was the address they had for it. I gave them the address and phone number of where she was. They said they would check there.

Yvonne phoned at the start of December, I think it was a Thursday but I can't be sure. She said she was out of the rehab centre, having been kicked out for fighting. She never told me where she was and I didn't ask.

A couple of days after that Yvonne turned up at my door with a new girlfriend Linda. Yvonne was fine and not stoned. She asked me if I had any money to give her but I told her I didn't and emptied out my purse to show her. That night Yvonne was fine, laughing. She couldn't have been any better. Her and Linda stayed the night, sleeping in the living room. That night Yvonne was fine and the next day I went to work after taking my son to school. I left Yvonne and Linda in the house telling Carolann to make sure they were gone before she left. That was the last I saw of her.

POLICE

Are you a Constable with Strathclyde Police?

Yes, sir.

In the early hours of Sunday the 8th of December last year were you called to the YMCA hostel in Renfrew?

Yes. sir.

Did you go there about half past one with a colleague of yours?

Yes, sir.

And did you meet a lady doctor who told you that she had been called to see a patient at the YMCA hostel in Renfrew?

Yes, sir.

Did the doctor indicate that because of the aggressive attitude of the patient she was unable to examine her?

Yes, sir.

Did you meet the patient?

Yes, I did.

Was that Yvonne Gilmour?

Yes.

And in the course of your meeting with her did she tell you that there was an outstanding warrant for her?

Yes, that's correct.

Did you check that?

My colleague did.

And did you discover that that in fact was correct?

Yes.

Do you remember the nature of the warrant?

It was an apprehension warrant issued by Glasgow Sheriff Court.

As a result of that warrant was Yvonne Gilmour arrested?

Yes.

Was she arrested in respect of anything that had happened in the YMCA that night?

It was solely in connection with the warrant, sir.

What was Yvonne Gilmour's behaviour like when you interviewed her at the YMCA?

Initially she was quite aggressive but eventually she calmed down. I spoke to her for a short time and she calmed down substantially.

Did you take her to Govan Police Office?

Yes.

If Yvonne hadn't told you that she had an outstanding warrant would you have thought to check it up?

I couldn't honestly say. I don't know whether we would have or not, probably not.[22]

PART THREE

Prison

The place where the deaths occurred is not a hospital, nor is it a girls' school. It is a Penal Institution. The inmates were not there to be cured or educated. They were there because they had been charged with offences and had been remanded in custody. They were not there willingly.

There was no particular reason why they should co-operate with the regime.

Determination by John Joseph Maguire, Queen's Counsel, Sheriff Principal of the Sheriffdom of Tayside Central and Fife in the Fatal Accident Inquiry into the deaths of Kelly Holland and Arlene Elliot, 8 March 1996
Determination by John Joseph Maguire, Queen's Counsel, Sheriff Principal of the Sheriffdom of Tayside Central and Fife in the Fatal Accident Inquiry into the deaths of Angela Bollan, Denise Anne Devine and Yvonne Gilmour, 18th November 1997

[The prison is] a cross between a psychiatric ward and a casualty clearing station.
[The inmates] are as disordered and deranged and damaged by drugs and alcohol as ever

Mr Clive Fairweather, Chief Inspector of Prisons, Scotland, 25th February 1999

It's just that being in prison is hellish for these girls, it's absolutely hellish. It may not be a hellish prison, but being in prison is hellish for these people.

Medical Officer, Cornton Vale. Transcript of Proceedings in Continued Fatal Accident Inquiry into the death of Angela Bollan and Others, 16th June 1997

Don't throw allegations over to me, right, because I'm no' throwing them to you about the fucking prison service, right. It stinks.
Cornton Vale inmate. Transcript of Proceedings in Continued Fatal Accident Inquiry into the death of Angela Bollan and Others, 10th March 1997

CHAPTER 8

Cornton Vale

UNIT MANAGER, CORNTON VALE

Cornton Vale is a prison which accommodates female prisoners of all categories. It houses adults and young offenders, untried and unsentenced prisoners and those who have received sentence. The total capacity in 1996 was 219, with an average occupancy of about 180. The administration block encloses the Prison gates and the reception and visiting areas. There is also a central block which includes workshops, a laundry, a cookhouse, the gymnasium and the educational department. There is also a multi-denominational chapel. There are 5 accommodation halls for prisoners. Remand prisoners were housed in what was then called Romeo Block. There are six units in the block, three on each of the two storeys, with 7 cells per unit so the design capacity for Romeo is 41 inmates with single cell occupation. Each unit also has a sitting room, a kitchen and showers. In some units, there was doubling-up of prisoners. When a cell was shared, a bunk-bed was provided. There was also a larger cell classed as a mother and baby room since from time to time we have to accommodate mothers with their small babies. Otherwise this larger cell sometimes housed three prisoners. Unit 1 housed the strict suicidal supervisions, the Triple S prisoners.

In the normal cells, there would be a cupboard for hanging individual items of clothing, there would be a small locker, there would be the bed obviously and there was a table top which would house a sink. The Triple S cells were very basic, just with their plumbing and a mattress on the floor.

The average number of hours prisoners spent out of their cells worked out at about just under 9 hours a day which compared quite favourably with other prisons when a survey was held.

Prisoners were let out of their cells in the morning within ten minutes or a quarter of an hour of the staff starting their shift which would be about quarter to seven roughly. They would then wash, receive medication and prepare and be served breakfast. They would be out until about quarter past eight when the first of the two split shift breakfasts for the staff started. While out, the prisoners were at liberty to go back to their cell or stay in the sitting room or visit other prisoners within the unit. The staff breaks lasted about one and a half to just under two hours. During this time the inmates would be in their cells unless they were called upon to go to a class or the gymnasium or the health centre to see the doctor. After the staff breaks they would be out of their cells until lock-up at lunch-time which could be two or three hours. The next lock-up would be for a staff changeover which could be anything between half an hour and two hours depending on the regime to be operated that day. The prisoners would be allowed out of their cells in the afternoon until lock-up at tea-time, in general, about 5 o'clock. There are sometimes operational reasons why inmates might be required to be locked in their cells. Remand prisoners, for example, receive visits in the afternoon three days a week which is staffed by remand staff, which would mean prisoners may be locked up from lunch until about three when visits are finished. Between five and six o'clock the staff go for their break so the prisoners would be in their cells again but then they are out till lock-up at nine o'clock.

Visits for social workers and canteen facilities three times a week are the other main times out of their cell. If staff is required to escort prisoners to these activities, it could affect time out of the cells for other inmates in that prisoners have to be secured in their cells if they are not involved in these activities.

There are not so many activities at the weekends, not so many visits from social workers and external visitors and there's no canteen at the weekend, so there is more time for out of cell association.

In prisons, in general, you can't generalise to say that that's the regime because of the type of prisoner, for example, that men get out less because they're more difficult to control. In times of bother, then the regime is restricted, in times of quietness it's relaxed.[23]

DEPUTY GOVERNOR, CORNTON VALE

Is there anything by way of a written timetable which is given to prisoners and which might give them an expectation as to the hours they can expect to be in association as opposed to being locked in their cells?

I'm not aware of such a specific document, no.

Has there been during the time that you have been at the prison any material alteration in the amount of time that prisoners in Romeo Block are allowed to have in association, as opposed to being in their own cells?

Only in the sense that we have asked staff to ensure that they are out for the maximum amount of time possible, but that obviously fluctuates on a day by day basis. I'm not aware of them being out more. I'm aware of them being out more in Cornton Vale than they are in other jails, but in Cornton Vale itself I think it's pretty stable in the sense that they are out of their accommodation areas and in the sitting rooms and out of the blocks as much as possible.

Who has the responsibility day to day for deciding how much time inmates are allowed to be in association?

Well, it's primarily determined by staffing numbers, and that would be the supervisor's responsibility primarily.

Does the supervising officer then have a certain amount of discretion in the amount of time that they can allow by way of association day to day?

They really have to, yes.

Depending on staffing levels, for example?

Yes, because if someone calls in sick, then they have to make last minute adjustments etc etc. It's very much dependent on staff availability.

Do you know whether or not there is any guidance or instruction given to supervisors as to how much association they should allow, given that they have staff up to complement?

> They have a direct instruction that they should try to have the prisoners out for the maximum amount of time possible.[24]

GOVERNOR, CORNTON VALE

The supervisor has responsibility for running the block. The supervisor is there to ensure that the rules and regulations, the normal operation of the block is effective. Senior management team manages by walking about. I and my senior management team are out around the establishment on a regular basis. We ask who is locked up, we ask what's going on in the block. That's perfectly normal and it's perfectly routine. There's a residential manager, the head of custodies does that, I do that personally. So that's a number of people who are checking, asking questions. There are other checks and balances. If you are suggesting, as I understand, that there is a potential for an abuse of that discretion, then if the prisoner herself feels that she has been treated unfairly, then she has the grievance procedure. She may write to her lawyer, she can contact her family, there are lots of ways for the prisoner to make it known that she's not satisfied with what's happening. So I am satisfied that the checks and balances that we have in place ensure that discretion is used with integrity and with professionalism.[25]

There isn't actually any positive right of association according to the rules, but we have a routine which means they are out of cell as much, or as often as possible throughout seven days a week, which is probably quite unique to Cornton Vale in my experience.

In my time as Governor, remand inmates spend more time out of their cells than other people. The time out has increased about two hours a day, longer at the weekends, probable three and a half, because routinely previously prisoners on remand were locked up at weekends after 5 o'clock. This has been achieved by the provision of an extra officer on each shift and also a commitment to the fact that if we have staff shortages for any reason that staff will be concentrated in the remand unit. They will be given priority in terms of full staffing.[26]

Can you tell us what the present state of affairs is vis-à-vis cell sharing for remand prisoners?

Those on the suicide prevention strategy are in single cells and the whole of the ground floor in the remand block is single cell accommodation. Upstairs it's shared accommodation. I prefer, where possible, that accommodation is shared. It helps where they are feeling particularly unhappy or confused or uncertain and if they have someone else there to support them, then it is quite good, so we try to do that as far as possible, but not downstairs, that's single cell accommodation.

If an inmate expresses a preference to have a single cell, will she be accommodated in one?

So long as we are happy that she is suitable for a single cell.

If inmates choose to share, will that always be possible?

Most of the time it will be possible, yes. Quite often women will ask to share with their friends, or sometimes to share with an older woman. It really varies quite a lot but if we can help them by putting them with someone that they know or like, or a friend or whatever, then we do that.[27]

MEDICAL OFFICER, CORNTON VALE

I feel conscious that I am not a hospital doctor and the general practitioner who comes to Cornton Vale needs a wide experience of problems, but it is a prison. ... We try to do our best because there isn't a more appropriate hospital to put them in. So we are in a catch 22 situation. I don't want to make Cornton Vale into a second rate hospital that uses staff that are not originally designed for that purpose, yet I don't want to have an environment that is not helpful and supportive and we must try and have some balance between the two.

Yes, because it is a prison with a hospital function, would you agree with that?

Well, the hospital part was taken away some time ago, so there is not a hospital unit in Cornton Vale. It is used as a dumping ground, not a hospital.[28]

CHAPTER 9

Prison Staff

PRISON OFFICER

You mentioned that there were staffing changes in 1990?

They were implementing quite a few changes all at the one time and one of them was bringing male staff into Cornton Vale and female staff moving out. When I first joined the service in 1978 it was totally female staff and now it's mixed.

And what effect did the change have on the morale of the female staff that had been there prior to 1990?

It was just unsettling because a lot of females were wanting to move out, so it was just getting settled back into your way of working.

So it was related to the fact that they were new staff and not to the fact that the new staff was male?

That's right.

As far as the interaction between female and male staff is concerned, do I understand that there's not a problem there so far as staff morale's concerned?

It's fine.

Do you think there would have been any difficulty so far as the female inmates were concerned that male staff were introduced?

A few prisoners can't cope with males just because of their life-style outside. A lot of women have been abused and they cannae really relate to male officers.

Are there also difficulties in relation to the question of privacy for females being looked after by males?

I can only speak for my own unit, no.

But it could be difficult if a male officer has to carry out observations on a female inmate during the night, for example?

Normally it's a female officer that's on the blocks during the night. That's the governor's policy. It's one of the changes she made.

And there might be a problem if the officer who was first on duty in the morning, there might be a problem with checking the prisoners first thing in the morning?

The normal policy is that the male officer chaps the door and gets an answer.

And so far as bathing and showering et cetera, it may be that females would be embarrassed if males were in the area. That may be a problem?

It could be.

But is it?

Not really. As I said, it's a separate section where the showers and toilets are and there are curtains up so it's no' an open area that they can look in and see the girls in the bath or the shower.

So if we want to understand what happens at Cornton Vale, are we to understand that the fact that there are men there looking after women, it doesn't cause any trouble?

None whatsoever.

Is the change to mixed staff a good thing or a bad thing from the point of view of running the prison?

I think it's quite healthy.

How has it affected the atmosphere in the prison?

I think it's given it a more normal atmosphere. I think it's natural, it's more like outside.[29]

PRISON NURSE

BY THE COURT: I wonder can you help me with regard to a kind of general thing. What's, I mean you came in to, dare I say, the prisons late in life, you had been working in the hospitals a bit before that. What's the atmosphere like in the prison, so far as you can see with regard to, say, the relationship between the officers and inmates?

I'd actually, as you correctly say, I had no involvement at all with the Prison Service and when I did come in I expected to find it a lot more different than I have found it.

Yes?

And I have been pleasantly surprised in fact as to what I found and I do believe that in general the relationship between the prison officers and the prisoners, the feeling on the whole is going towards helping rather than just custodial care.

Well, is that reciprocated? I mean, what's the attitude of the prisoners towards the staff?

It's not always reciprocated.

I suppose that's understandable, they don't particularly want to be there?

That's correct.

And do they make that clear on occasion?

They certainly do, sometimes to ourselves, yes.[30]

DEPUTY GOVERNOR

You have told us that part of your job as a manager is to walk around the prison?

Yes.

Do you actually physically do that?

Yes, I try to go round at least once a day and I instruct my other managers to do that.

And when you are walking around the prison, do you see both staff and prisoners?

Yes.

Do you talk to people?

Yes.

Do you know, do the prisoners, so far as you can tell, seem to talk to residential staff?

In my judgement the relationships are excellent. There are always staff talking to prisoners and prisoners having a banter with staff or staff interviewing prisoners for particular reasons.[31]

GOVERNOR

Certainly in my experience of Cornton Vale ... the relationship, and that's something we picked up as inspectors earlier on in '96, the relationship between staff and prisoners at Cornton Vale is probably among the best kind of relationship that I have seen in my experience with working in lots of establishments across the service. Women will speak to prison officers without any difficulties, will share a lot about themselves and about their families and they do that with trust. I think they know that we share a lot of sensitive and confidential information and they trust us with that information.[32]

PRISON MEDICAL OFFICER

...one of the first things I observed going round the prison was that the windows of the offices were festooned with thank you cards. They had letters pinned up with photographs of the inmates' children and it was as far from the, you know, Prisoner Cell Block H sort of attitude as I could believe. ... There was an independent study that was carried out at the Governor's request and a lot of prisoners were interviewed and a lot of staff were interviewed and they were both asked how they felt about their relationships with each other and over 90 per cent of the prisoners rated the staff relationships very highly and about 92 per cent I think of the prison officers rated their relationships as very good, so that's the vast majority of both prisoners and officers.[33]

INMATE (30 YEARS OLD)

I've been in Cornton Vale about thirty times in total and I've never seen any officer act in the way that he did. I know I have a bad attitude but I never had any problems with any prison officer like we had with him. Most of the officers in Cornton Vale are really good. He's one of the few the girls don't like.[34]

PRISON OFFICER

At the shift handover, we get details on the prisoners. We go through every inmate and we'll say that Jane had a good day,

Irene was up and down, she had a bad letter, but she's okay, she's spoke to someone about it and she's okay, this one has found out she's pregnant and she's not so happy, or she is happy, actually, a full breakdown on every prisoner that I have got to cell, that I'm in charge of that night.[35]

CHAPTER 10

The Inmates

PROFESSOR OF PSYCHIATRY

I think one of the worst experiences that we have to offer people in our society is to send them to prison ... in spite of the fact that prisons do their best to ameliorate the inevitable horror of it all.

The biggest problem about going to prison is that freedom and liberty are taken away. The choices that one makes in ordinary everyday life are gone. Everything has to be organised by somebody else and there are various things one can and can't do, and we cherish our ability to choose what we do, and even if we are at times constrained we know that's coming to an end at a particular point, whereas a prisoner can't say that's going to end until the end of their sentence.[36]

VISITING MEDICAL OFFICER

They are often in a very chaotic state when they arrive with us and they will very often have been using drugs heavily. They have often got backgrounds of previous suicide attempts and depressive illnesses and of lots of other problems, such as abuse at home, and they will often have been in the prison for 24 hours or more without either drugs or medication, and their initial period of time in prison they may indeed be very brittle and very difficult to assess in terms of particular behaviour.[37]

GOVERNOR

I'm sad to say that it is not unusual for women to come to Cornton Vale who really don't understand what is happening to them and it can take them a long time to speak. Sometimes they are not able to speak at all, it just depends on what condition they arrive in at the prison. So some interviews with some women who are compos mentis and quite sensible can take a comparatively short length of time, others take a long time because the women are so unwell.[38]

PRISONER SUPERVISOR

And for me to get the information that I'm looking for I've got to deal with them all individually because they are all individuals. Those who work with me, we all realise it and it's a standing joke, how many hats have you had on that day, because you are dealing with disturbed prisoners, you are dealing with very intelligent prisoners, you are dealing with completely uneducated prisoners, aggressive prisoners, passive prisoners, and the remand population is so diverse, I don't think there is any other place that would have so many different personalities enclosed in one area.

Prisoners are often very confused about why they have been remanded. They sometimes don't understand why they're with us. In a lot of cases, and I know I'm generalising, but in a lot of cases, they will say, 'But my lawyer told me I'd get out.' It's such a stressful time that some information is absorbed and some isn't. I can have women who are in an extremely confused state and extremely upset. When I interview someone on admission, I'm looking to see how she is coping. I think in all honesty that we know that they are all vulnerable. I think we've learned that over the past two years that all admissions that are coming in are vulnerable, but I'm looking to see how she is coping with it herself. One of the things that I'll always find out initially is, is there something going to really worry you tonight. You know, where are your kids, is your house secure, is everything okay, is there something that is going to stop you sleeping tonight that I could be dealing with now. And there are a lot of cases like that. It can be, for example, children. That's the biggest thing. They've maybe got two kids, one is 14 the other is 10 and the 14 year old has been left in charge because there is no-one else. Or it's small children who are being looked after by a neighbour because the mother expected to get out from Court that day, so this neighbour has now inherited her children and the mother is worried. It can be things like my dog's locked in the house, who's going to feed it, that type of thing.[39]

PRISON MEDICAL OFFICER

Inmates are often referred to me by staff who might see some cause for concern. ... It's usually something that has happened outside the jail, it's usually a bad visit, bad news from home, family getting taken into care, social workers involved with the children. It's nearly always something outwith the prison that happens in a patient's personal life. ... Many of the patients I have get bad news all the time.[40]

That's what makes prison so intolerable for prisoners. I think that's what they find so intolerable, being in this position of powerlessness and all these things that are devastating are happening on the outside and they can do very little about it.[41]

VISITING MEDICAL OFFICER

Somewhere around two-thirds of the patients we see will have drug problems on admission and I can't give you an exact percentage but it would be a very common picture to have a history of mental illness, to have a history of suicide attempt, to have a history of physical or sexual abuse in childhood, to have a history of broken homes, this is a very common picture in the drug-using population who form two-thirds of our admissions.[42]

GOVERNOR

... a lot of women who come to us are really very unwell indeed. ... they are often poly drug abusers, they are often very poorly, physically and emotionally, and if we can be sure that we are focusing the resources that we have effectively, that we are assessing needs effectively and addressing them quickly, both in terms of medication and personal support, then I hope that will have a ripple effect in the way that they feel about themselves in general because quite often these women have extremely low self-esteem too and it's terribly important to raise that self-esteem, and if they feel better physically and mentally, then we have a good chance of building that up. ... Part of the difficulty we have is that they are with us for such a short time. It's very difficult to do anything constructive with women who are only with us for less than three weeks, which is the average length of stay on remand.[43]

PRISON SUPERVISOR

We have heard, for instance, that there is often bad language used by prisoners, and indeed sometimes by prison officers?

That's correct, yes.

And we've looked at some letters which show that some people habitually swear, is that right?

Well, yes, yes, that's true.

And would you agree that that applies to some prisoners, applies to some prison officers and it applies to lots of people just in the outside world?

It applies to society in general.

Yes. And so we can take it that using bad language in itself is just nothing out of the ordinary at all?

It's nothing unusual, no.

And can we also assume that most people who are sent to prison either on remand or indeed, to serve a sentence, don't want to be there?

I would think that the majority don't want to be there.

You told us that occasionally if someone has a bad visit then afterwards everything will be your fault?

We have found that visits, letters, telephone calls, something that just doesn't go the way a prisoner would like it to go, the first person that's going to get it is the unit officer, or myself, whoever happens to be there.

And can you describe what you mean by 'getting it', what are you thinking of?

You can get a lot of verbal abuse, you can get physical abuse as well. They know the procedures that will come into place if they attack you physically so they maybe go for the fabric of the building, kicking doors, walls, throwing things about and it's just general disorder.

And so while one no doubt would not expect the prison to be in a state of disorder from day to day, are there sometimes occasions when people, prisoners that is, do damage things within the prison because they are frustrated about something?

Yes.

And in the course of doing that might they say to you in more colourful language than I'll use, it's your fault, you're keeping me here and I should be back home?

Well, if I don't get the blame, then the courts get the blame, the police get the blame, the Sheriffs get the blame, it's everybody's fault but their own.[44]

INMATE (26 YEARS OLD)

You've been in Cornton Vale on a number of occasions?

Yes, a number of times, for shoplifting.

When the girls are talking together what kind of things do they talk about?

Everything, a bit of everything. Sometimes people talk about drugs, about what they're gonnae do when they get out, whether they're gonnae try and get their life sorted, they talk about their kids, the majority of them have got kids, what ages, show photies, just general things.

Yes?

What's been on the tele.

So that's your local life you are talking about but when they're talking about the future, what kind of things do the girls say to each other with regard to drugs, with regard to the future, with regard to not offending again?

Some would say, well, I've been taking drugs all these years, it's too hard now to try and stop. Other ones will say, I'm willing to give it a try. They say I'm gonnae try ma hardest, after I get out from this remand, then I'm gonnae give it a try and try and stay off drugs. But others are just past it, they've just gave up.[45]

INMATE (18 YEARS OLD)

You are only 18, is that right?

Yes.

And you've been in the prison a few times?

Yes.

Do people in the prison feel that they've been in, they know they are going to go out and back on drugs and will be back in again?

Yes.

A kind of depressing future maybe?

Yes.

And the families know that that happens that their daughter or wife or whoever is in the prison, out again, back in again?

No, it doesn't surprise them.

Is that because families of people addicted to drugs know that it's not going to be easy getting them off drugs forever?

No, it's no' that they don't, it's they know that you are going to be back in the jail again.[46]

CHAPTER 11

Drug Withdrawals

PRISON OFFICER

Now you've been in Cornton Vale for a really long time?

Yes, I've been an officer there for nineteen years.

Have you seen the population or the type of population change since 1978?

Drastically.

Could you tell us what way the picture has changed since 1978?

In years gone by it was mostly offences for prostitution or drink. Nowadays in the majority of prisoners it's all drug-related offences they're in for and quite a lot of them look in quite a poor state of health.

Age-wise, has the picture changed since 1978 with regard to the age of the inmates?

The average age for the prisoners is usually between say about twenty or thirty. You get very few older prisoners in, very few.

At the bottom end, are there very few?

Very few. I think in the whole prison you'd maybe be looking at eight or nine young offenders.

You've been in this prison for the best part of twenty years, and it's only in the last couple of years that there's been this tremendous incidence of people committing suicide. Have you thought, at all, either by yourself or along with your colleagues, as to what might have been causing this?

I just assume it's the type of drugs they're taking outside. I don't know.

You must have thought about this question?

When we ask the prisoners when they first get admitted if

they've got a drug habit, they usually tell us the type of drugs they're taking and it's never usually one drug, it's always a cocktail of three or four different drugs they take.

Yes, and how are you relating that to the fact that while they're in prison, while they're presumably on drugs reduction, that they are committing suicide when they are in prison? What is the exact relationship that you are drawing here?

I don't really know.

Well, is it the fact that while in prison they are not taking this cocktail of drugs you described?

They do get medication from the health centre to put them on reduction programmes.

So they are on a reduction programme?

Yes.

Are you drawing any relationship between the fact that they are on a drug reduction programme and that they were taking a large number of drugs outside?

Yes.

Can you tell me what connection it is that you are making between these two factors?

I think when they come in at first, that the amount of drugs they've been taking outside, then they get the reduction when they come into prison, it's a big, big change.

Now I don't want to put words into your mouth but do you observe that it is hard for them to cope with that reduction?

Quite a percentage, yes.

Yes, and is that the connection that you are making between the suicides that have taken place.

I never said that.[47]

PRISON SUPERVISOR

The withdrawals that we've seen inside Cornton Vale are horrific.[48]

PRISON SUPERVISOR

Well, some of the girls will tell you they have withdrawal symptoms like sore stomachs, the shakes even if they don't, as a ploy to get more medication. It's quite common for some of the girls to have maybe used the telephone, come away from the telephone crying and say that their mother or father, somebody's in the hospital, their child's been knocked down and then they have a weeping fit. We contact the health centre and this is them looking to get something to help them through the night or help them through the day or whatever. It's quite common. When we've actually checked out these stories and sometimes it's the parents we're phoning and we say so-and-so tells us their dad's been taken to hospital. Can you tell us what condition he's in and he's no' in the hospital, he's sitting here. That happens fairly frequently.[49]

INMATE (18 YEARS OLD)

BY THE COURT: Can you tell us really what life was like in Cornton Vale? I mean, the realities of it for somebody like you who has been in and out a couple of times, and so on, and you are coming back again. What do people feel?

It gets harder every time.

And the set up in the prison, is that hard in the sense of being physically hard, or is it hard more in the sense of being, there isn't much to do when you are left a lot to your own devices, or what?

There really isnae much to do but it doesn't drive you to suicide.

And are your times in prison connected with drugs, the reasons why you are inside connected with drugs in any way?

Yes.

Is that true of just a small number of the girls, or a lot of the girls, or all of the girls?

Most of them.

Did you find the period after you went in, that's just to say the

fortnight or so after you went into the prison, difficult with regard to not having the drugs?

Yes.

In a sense is the period on remand, is it better or worse than actually serving a sentence in any of the other blocks?

It's worse because you don't know when you are up at Court, well, you know, when you are up at Court, but you don't know what's going to happen at Court.

Yes?

There's nothing to do all day.

And how about from the drugs situation, or the not having the drugs situation?

Everybody is in the same boat that way.

All of those who are on drugs are coming off drugs, or on withdrawal, are they?

Yes.

And is that, does that make the remand block more unpleasant than anywhere else, this kind of withdrawal thing from drugs?

Sometimes, because more people go on to the remand and then go to get convicted than go straight to convicted, so there's more people on remand.

And when you talk about problems outside, what are you thinking about, what will the girls be thinking about?

How they are going to get their next hit and things like that.

How about things like, well, if they had any babies, for example?

Aye, if they had kids, maybe weans and things like that.

But your first answer to my question was that they were worried about their next fix?

Worried that they couldnae get drugs, they couldnae cope without drugs.

And what about diazepam, does that help?

No' really, no.

Does it not?

They take you off too quick.

You say they take you off too quick, is the 'it' whatever drugs you are on, or the diazepam?

Diazepam and dihydrocodeine.

Are you saying that so far as you are concerned, the system turns the tap off a bit too quickly?

Yes.[50]

PRISON MEDICAL OFFICER

Until I became Medical Officer, there were three different regimes for the prescription of diazepam for inmates. The material difference between them was the amount of the drug prescribed on a day-to-day basis over a four-week period. Now there is a single regime, using a combination of dihydrocodeine and diazepam for everyone. Dihydrocodeine is a long-acting preparation of an opiate replacement. The same amount for the same period of time, four weeks, is prescribed to all inmates. There are a few exceptions but by and large we stick to it. I changed to this regime because I think it's more appropriate to treat people with opiate addictions with an opiate, in this case dihydrocodeine. The problem with the different quantity regime is in doing your assessment one strives to get the best information and you ask the patient concerned when you first meet her at the medical and I refer to the nurses admission profile – I want to know if people's drug use has changed, have they perhaps not been telling the absolute truth on admission. But I'm afraid it's very difficult to get personal assessment of people's drug-taking, not just because they are lying but because it varies from day to day. Not everybody takes the same every day and it's very difficult to get an accurate assessment. And one of the things that causes problems in the prison is if you are not consistent and one patient is getting more than someone else. In the light of these difficulties it seems more straightforward and perhaps more fair to prescribe the same for all and that is based on an amount which hopefully would do no harm if you give it to someone who had lied and had not taken drugs at all but at the same time would cope with the major symptoms of drug withdrawal. It would be generally accepted, I think, that 60mls a day would prevent convulsions so we picked on that regime for that reason.[51]

MEDICAL PROFESSOR

We have heard that dihydrocodeine is an opiate, an opiate replacement. Can you explain to me in terms a lay person will understand, what diazepam is for?

Diazepam is a minor tranquilliser and it has the effect of reducing distress, reducing anxiety and reducing agitation in most individuals.

You will have heard of patients telling you that they buy valium and that they take it in much bigger quantities than you would ever prescribe to anyone?

Yes, I mean even in prison we are prescribing it at something like four times the recommended daily therapeutic dose.[52]

Diazepam is a benzodiazepine. There is very clear evidence that this group of drugs, which are effectively what we call the minor tranquillisers, apart from their dependency problems, also have a problem in that they can diminish one's resolve not to undertake a suicide act. In other words, it weakens one's ability to cope. The example I would give is that sometimes people put on benzodiazepines do things like shoplifting which, you know, they would not normally do if they were not being given benzodiazepines. All the effects are not positive, they can be negative. Sometimes people on benzodiazepines can even become quite aggressive, a paradoxical effect. So, although it's very useful in sedating the individual, assisting them in coping with the withdrawal symptoms to be calmer and more tranquil, in some instances I think it can lead to a weakening of resolve to continue. It can cause enhanced despair. It can have a depressing effect.[53]

PRISON MEDICAL OFFICER

Benzodiazepines are a drug with a lot of problems and certainly don't always calm people down. In some people, they become the opposite, they become more argumentative, more difficult, and they also inhibit your control mechanisms, so perhaps someone who had some benzodiazepines may lose some of the control mechanisms that they would normally have and be disinhibited and think 'Well, what is there to live for?' That's perfectly possible The only reason we prescribe benzodiazepines is because most of the people we have coming in are probably drug misusers and if someone had a convulsion and we haven't got them on absolute observation overnight, they could die. I think basically it's the lesser of two evils but they are far from perfect drugs and I'm not saying they haven't got major side effects and major problems, they do, but we are sometimes stuck with what do you do when someone comes in who has been injecting temazepam plus taking a bit of this and a bit of that. It's a judgement we make but all these things go round in cycles. Some of the drugs we used to withdraw people ten years ago were regarded as ridiculous ten years ago and are now coming back into fashion and they have all had their use. For inmates who have a history of drug abuse which doesn't include benzodiazepines, I might modify the regime and I might offer them something to help them sleep at night. But one would try not to use benzodiazepines and certainly you wouldn't start someone on benzodiazepines who hadn't used them or misused them previously.[54]

INMATE (18 YEARS OLD)

Now, is it the case that in the prison when you first get admitted you are put on a drug regime?

Yes.

If you have taken drugs outwith the prison?

Yes.

And could you tell me please what your view of the sufficiency of the drugs that you are given to help you cope with your drug withdrawal if you are coming off, for example, methadone?

I don't think it's enough. I don't think they give you enough and they cut you down too quick.

So first of all, you get a dosage when you first come into prison and your view is that they don't give you enough?

Yes.

And then what they do is they reduce the dose and you are saying that that happens too suddenly?

It does. They cut you down too quickly, especially if you are coming off methadone, because at that time it hasn't really hit you yet, the withdrawals haven't even hit you.

And could it be the case that you are going to be hit with the withdrawal symptoms at a stage when your drugs have been reduced to the minimum?

Yes.

Is it something that you talk about in the prison?

Yes.

And what is it that is generally said about the drug regime?

What do we usually say?

Yes.

It's a load of crap.[55]

VISITING MEDICAL OFFICER

I think it's difficult for any of us to know how reliable their account is. We do very often find discrepancies in their reported prescribed medication when we check with GPs so we certainly know that they do not always tell the truth about their drug consumption, and there are often discrepancies between what is told to the nurse officer and then is told to us the following day, which sometimes would indicate that after having spoken to other prisoners, they'd say if they mention other drugs or bigger intakes they may get more drugs from us. So stories do change and I think it is difficult to take at face value what the actual intake is. And in fact our response to the quantity rather than the quality of drugs remains the same. This is part of the strategy that the withdrawal regime is a standard regime whether they come in on a quarter of a gram or one gram of heroin, and that means that all of the girls know what they will be getting and we don't see patients coming up to say 'She gets more than me' or 'I should get more than her' and that means we have a blanket policy. We can cover to a certain extent the possibility that some patients are not telling us exactly what they are taking. We can encompass in what we give enough medication to cover most eventualities.[56]

PRISON NURSE

If, for instance, we have heard evidence that a great number of the women who come to Cornton Vale Prison are drug abusers, then in order to deal with their drug abuse does the prison have to do what it can within the time that the person is with the prison?

That's most certainly the situation, yes.

And as a nurse you will know that in the outside world people will attend their GP for many months and indeed years in connection with drug abuse?

That's correct.

And at Cornton Vale are a number of the drug abusers who come into the prison there for a matter of days?

Absolutely.

And some for a matter of weeks

That's correct.

And no doubt some for months, and will some be there for years?

That's correct.

Are there quite a large number of the prisoners who are there for a short time in the context of getting off drugs?

Yes, there's a certain population that comes in and out frequently.

His Lordship has referred to a revolving door syndrome, which I understand him to mean not only that people come in, but also that they come in, go out and come back again?

That's very much the case with this group of prisoners, yes.

And of course, Cornton Vale is a prison, it is not a detoxification clinic or rehabilitation clinic, is it?

It certainly isn't.

BY THE COURT: When you are dealing with these girls are you trying to wean them off drugs, or are you just trying to maintain them alive, or what?

When the girls come in they are all put on the same detoxification programme, but the problem is if they are only in for a brief period then they have only been on that programme for a short time, and the questions arises...

I mean, if they are on remand for say reports, for three weeks or something of that sort, is that, I mean, in your practised view, is there really any point in trying to get them off drugs during that period?

That's an issue that has really to be addressed, yes, I think that is a problem.[57]

PRISON MEDICAL OFFICER

I am a doctor and I can diagnose things. I can perhaps treat some illnesses and perhaps prevent others, but I cannot possibly change a whole system. I have to remain focused in what I as a doctor can achieve in Cornton Vale within the prison system, but I want it to be as humane a place as possible, and these are my patients.[58]

GOVERNOR

I don't see that a drug withdrawal unit would be helpful to us. In any one day we can probably have an average of about 30 women who are undergoing drug withdrawal protocol that our medical officer introduced. That would be a combination of remand and short-term convicted women. It would need to be a very large unit to accommodate the number of women who may have drug difficulties. We're well aware of the difficulties in drug withdrawal in the remand population. The effect on the mental and physical well-being of the women since our medical officer introduced his style of drug withdrawal is much better than existed previously when drug-induced seizures were the norm and a lot of women suffered from diarrhoea and sickness... I can see that the women's health is much better. We also have for their support psychiatric and psychological intervention. We have an addictions worker, and we have staff who understand the difficulties ... and we have 24 hour care in the establishment. I think in the circumstances that probably is a very reasonable response to the needs. My view is that if they need intensive therapy, if they are so ill that they need intensive nursing support and care, then prison is not the place for them.[59]

CHAPTER 12

Methadone in Prison

MEDICAL OFFICER

Methadone may well flatten emotions, yes. It doesn't give you the same high or the same euphoria that taking opiates gives, which is why some people will top up with it, some people prefer that, but it's reported to give you a sense of well-being, like a warm feeling, like maybe hot soup on a cold day in your stomach, a somewhat warm feeling that exudes out.[60]

INMATE (19 YEARS OLD)

You said that you had been in prison over a number of years, in Cornton Vale Prison, is that right?

Aye.

You must understand that if you nod, then your answer won't be recorded. So I appreciate it's easier for you to nod, but we've all got to note your actual answers, so it's easier if you say yes or no, or give a full answer. Do you understand that?

Aye, ah didnae know it wis gettin' recorded.

It's not that we're trying to be difficult, it's just that we do have to hear your answer. So for how long have you been in and out of Cornton Vale, can you help us with that?

Three years.

And during your time in the prison, you would get to know the other prisoners quite well, the regular prisoners, is that right?

Aye.

And you would also then get to know the new prisoners who came in?

Aye.

Were there a lot of prisoners who had problems with drugs?

Aye. Ninety per cent of Cornton Vale Prison's drug abusers.

So most of the girls coming into the prison are having to deal with the fact that they're coming off drugs?

Aye.

Because obviously once they're sentenced or remanded they're not going to have accesss to the drugs that they have when they're at liberty?

Aye.

So that would be a problem that you've encountered?

Aye.

Because you use drugs, don't you?

Aye.

So when you're locked up you don't have access to the drugs that you do on the streets so you've got to cope without them?

Aye.

And lots of other girls have got to do that as well?

Aye.

Now you said that you were coming off heroin?

Aye, that's right.

Is that the only drug you've taken or do you have to cope with coming off other drugs?

Just heroin.

Have you ever had to cope with coming off methadone, for example?

Aye, but no' in jail, no' inside.

When in your past have you had to cope with coming off methadone?

When ah wis fifteen, sixteen, ah done it twice.

And in what circumstances did you have to come off?

Ah jist wanted off it.

And how did you react to stopping taking the methadone?

Ah wis taking dihydrocodeine to substitute, see ah'm comin' aff it but ah ended up addicted tae them.

Did you find they helped you much?

It's jist aff o' wan an' ontae another, that's whit happened.

Did you find that in coming off the methadone it was worse at the beginning or did it start to get bad later on?

Ye can stop takin' yer methadone, right, an' see four weeks later, that's when ye come doon wi' a bang, that's when it hits ye.

So it's after a period of four weeks that ....?

Ye're awright fir four weeks and then it hits ye.

Hits you with a bang, you said?

Aye. Eats intae yer bones an' everythin', ye hallucinate, everythin' happens.

Now you've used this expression 'eats into your bones'. I don't understand what you mean by that. Can you explain what it means?

Ye've got see, aw yer joints, behind yer calves an' a' that, it makes ye twitch, it jist eats away at ye.

Is that the feeling ...?

Ye've got tae dae that a' the time.

And what you're doing in the witness box there is you're showing quick jerky movements with your arm and your shoulder. And that's part of the symptoms of coming off methadone?

Aye.

And that happens after four weeks?

Aye.

Have you seen girls in the Prison coming off methadone reacting in the same way?

See, when ye're gawn tae yer bed it's really bad, but during the day, ye don't twitch.

But at night time...?

Ah don't know how it works like that, but when yer gawn tae sleep comin' aff any drug, that's when it really starts tae hit ye, when ye're tryin' tae go tae sleep.

So you're saying that the time it hits you most when you're coming off drugs is when you're in your bed at night?

Lyin' doon, wherever.

Now the question I originally asked you was whether or not you'd been able to see other girls in the prison experiencing these types of withdrawal symptoms?

No' as bad, naw.

Not as bad?

Wan lassie, she's deid now. Ah seen her in the cells in the Sheriff Court in Glasgow. She wis pure hallucinating an a' that comin' aff the methadone. That's why ah don't want tae go on the methadone. It's harder comin' aff. It's bad enough comin' aff the heroin.

Do you know what sort of help was available for people like you who were suffering from withdrawal symptoms?

Whit, fae methadone?

Methadone or ...?

Wance ye go inside the jail, right, ye get through reception, ye see the nurse and then they take yer details, whit drugs ye're on an a' that and the next day ye see the doctor. Ye don't get nuthin' the first night ye're in. Ye go tae see the doctor in the mornin' an' they put ye on four yellow valium, but that's like two blue valium ye get aff yer ain doctor ootside.

Are the blue or the yellow stronger?

The blue's stronger. But ye don't get yellow wans aff the doctor ootside, it's always blue wans ye get. They put it up tae two o' the dihydrocodeine and six yellow valium.

Do you get any methadone?

Naw, but a' the pregnant lassies get it.

So if you've been taking methadone outside and you come into prison, you don't get methadone in the prison?

Only if yer pregnant.

But you do get something to help you when you're in prison?

> Aye, but it disnae always help. So you go back tae the doctor an' say it's no' helpin' me but ye jist have tae take whit ye get but as soon as there's a hangin' it goes up, an' up, an' up, an' up.[61]

MEDICAL PROFESSOR

When I was involved as a medical officer in 1982 we abandoned the use of methadone. We had used methadone up to that time for the very rare individuals who came in as addicts. So I am not against methadone in principle and indeed I've used it partly with patients in my own general practice. However, we made a decision in '82 to stop using methadone and introduced a withdrawal regime at that time only with diazepam and subsequently now with dihydrocodeine and diazepam. I'm of the view that withdrawal from opiates, whether methadone or heroin, is going to lead to a problem in the withdrawal phase. People are going to have mental health problems even when you cover it, however adequately, with dihydrocodeine and diazepam. They are going to have a difficult time. I think if somebody is on a contract with the community addiction team, either a specialist team or their general practitioner, to receive methadone as a method of controlling their drug addiction and they are then admitted for a brief period on remand of less than a month or six weeks, and that's the majority of prisoners, then I think methadone should in fact be continued during that time. There are some caveats to that. What we find is that a number of the inmates who are on methadone are in fact breaking their contracts by taking illegally acquired drugs in addition, and I think that maybe needs to be addressed separately, but as a general rule if it is a very short admission, then withdrawing them for say two weeks on a dihydrocodeine and diazepam regime, then sending them back out, I don't think it's particularly helpful.

I think that methadone maintenance in the community is useful in one respect in that it often decriminalises the situation. Patients who have been on methadone substitution for eight, nine, ten years and are certainly getting on with their lives and are not criminals, to interrupt that for two weeks on remand I think is inappropriate.[62]

YVONNE'S GP

If you had a patient, doctor, who was on a long-term methadone prescription and she went into prison for say three weeks, would you have any reservation about continuing her methadone prescription to cover that three-week period so that she could have the methadone in prison, if that option was open to you?

The only thing I would want to ensure was that there was good communication between the GP, the pharmacist, the prison medical service, but if that were happening, then other than that I don't think I would have any reservations. We must make absolutely certain that we are all talking about the same patient and that we know what dose of methadone she was on, when she last had it, so that we will know how to continue it, and also whenever she left the prison that there should be communication to us so that it could be continued at an appropriate time.

And if the period were three months instead of three weeks?

I don't think that's really a question for me, but from my point of view if it were three months, I wouldn't have any objection to it. I wouldn't see a problem with it, but in a period of three months with someone in an environment where they are not going to have access to illicit drugs, by and large, then there might be a potential for doing something a bit more than just maintaining on methadone. It might be a good opportunity to try a drug reduction programme, but that would depend on people's motivation as well.

Do you see any clear benefit to somebody who has been on a methadone programme and who is remanded in prison for three weeks being kept on methadone while they are there?

I think there is some benefit in that the person would feel more secure knowing that they were getting their usual methadone. During the period in jail, they wouldn't have the opportunity to top up with illicit drugs, even if they had been doing that prior to coming in, so you would expect it would give them a three-week run just on methadone and we would know how they were doing and it would also avoid the need to restabilise them when they came out.[63]

MEDICAL OFFICER

Methadone is a very dangerous drug. It is tremendously useful, but without proper checks it can become a very dangerous drug, especially if someone tops it up with other drugs, and I had to be very, very sure of anybody who came in before I would take a chance on prescribing methadone for them. I make every effort to continue a methadone prescription for those who have been on methadone programmes outwith the prison if there is no sign of them abusing non-prescribed drugs. I have done that for almost all the patients we have seen who have come in stable on a methadone programme If you look at the database we fill in of drug misusers, there were about 58 people who were taking methadone who came in, but there were actually only 8 of those who were taking methadone and nothing else. The eight who were on methadone and stable I did not withdraw, even although we do not have a formal methadone programme.

Just to be clear about this, doctor, it may be that some of us have been under the misapprehension that methadone is not prescribed at all in Cornton Vale? Are you saying that that's not right?

That's not right.

Would inmates who told the nurse on admission that they had been topping up be ruled out for the continuation of methadone in prison?

Not necessarily. Sometimes they might tell the nurse they have been topping up for other reasons. They might think they might get more, or if they say they were using extra drugs to what they were getting prescribed. They may think that will lead us to give them a bigger prescription. If I was going to prescribe methadone, I only do it under incredibly straight check-up precautions. I don't just phone the GP. I ask them to fax me something back in return to make certain that what the patients say is accurate. I also want to know how long they've been stable for. I also want to know how clean their urine tests have been and have urine tests been done. Without the proper checks in prison, we really thought we shouldn't be prescribing methadone at all, but there are certain patients who come in sometimes for old warrants and old charges who have put their lives together, and if you like, I put my neck out for those, but I have to justify it to a body like this, if something went wrong and they topped up and died. So I have to be very sure about these patients.

The concern would be that somehow they would have access to non-prescribed drugs in Cornton Vale and they would take that in addition to the methadone and thereby harm themselves?

That's the main concern, but also if they give the methadone to another prisoner who wasn't using methadone. What can be a therapeutic dose for one person can be a lethal dose for somebody else.[64]

INMATE (18 YEARS OLD)

Do you agree that coming off drugs, whether it's voluntary, as you've tried in the past, or whether it is because you are in prison, is always going to be a difficult thing to do?

Definitely.

Because there are physical symptoms which are horrible, aren't they?

Yes.

And there's also the mental symptoms which are horrible too?

The mental symptoms you've got to watch.

You will be aware that people outside of prison can have methadone prescribed for getting off heroin?

Yes.

But you know that methadone can be addictive too, don't you?

Methadone is worse.[65]

INMATE (27 YEARS OLD)

There are physical symptoms and there are psychological symptoms?

Yes.

Could you help us briefly with the type of psychological symptoms that one would get in drug withdrawal?

Well, each case would obviously be different but just the craving to get some and feel normal again, because you don't feel normal, whatever normal is, but you don't feel very nice at all when you've not had it.

From your own experience, have you used methadone in the past?

Yes.

And have you ever had to go through methadone withdrawal?

Yes, when I was on a methadone prescription and I am currently still, and I went into prison then, it was the day Denise died before my withdrawals really hit me so that was like two weeks.

So when you were in Cornton Vale you had previously been taking methadone and you had to go through withdrawal when you were in the prison?

Yes.

And were you put on an automatic drug regime within the prison?

A couple of dihydrocodeine and a couple of valium twice a day.

And did you feel they were sufficient so far as you were concerned?

No, that's nothing really.

And when you say that it hit you, what was it you felt like?

Cold sweats, nausea, like sore limbs, withdrawal pains.

Yes?

Depression.

And what was it you were focusing on when you were depressed as a result of the withdrawal symptoms?

Well, previously I had been involved in an abduction of me, and I used to focus on the guy that done it, not giving in to him.

I wonder if you were focusing on your life in general and things that had happened to you outwith the prison?

Yes, I used to focus on never coming back to that prison, never, and trying to get my life in order. I went through a helluva ordeal and like they were asking me after Denise died if I was suicidal and I says no, if I was going to have done it, I would have done it years ago when that happened.[66]

CHAPTER 13

Suicide in Prison

PROFESSOR OF PSYCHIATRY

I do think that suicide is the tip of the iceberg and that there is a lot of mental distress in prisons which could be assisted with better services.[67]

CLINICAL PSYCHOLOGIST

The prediction of such a rare event of suicide on the basis of known risk factors remains difficult and the individual risk factors remain only weakly predictive.[68]

GOVERNOR

When prisoners are under stress, it is something that can lead them to become suicidal?

Yes, it can do. It is a factor.

And that's why you have procedures in place so that a prisoner under stress can be monitored because of that very real danger?

Yes, and also for careful prison management. I don't proceed on the assumption that everyone who suffers from stress is likely to commit suicide, but it's important to the management of a prisoner that those who are dealing with her are aware of a variety of pressures on her.

Because we have heard evidence that being in prison in itself is a stress for the inmate?

Absolutely, yes.

So any additional stress, whatever the cause, is something that would be a matter of concern?

That's right, because some prisoners handle stress and the business of being in prison extremely well, others do not. It's important to know which prisoners to watch.[69]

BY THE COURT: Were there sufficient incidents of suicidal or para-suicidal acts to really enable you to use the phrase 'routinely'?

Yes.

There are enough?

Yes, yes my Lord.[70]

PRISON NURSE

I believe in the group of prisoners that we are discussing, who come into the prison frequently with a fairly severe drug habit, when they arrive in reception probably the thing that's foremost in their mind and prevents them thinking more clearly about their life is their physical state and their well-being, because they come in, perhaps starting to withdraw, they are often in a poor state of health and the physical feeling takes over their thoughts at that time, and how they are going to get through the withdrawal and whether they are going to be given the medication. After they've been on the withdrawal programme for a period of two or three weeks the mental state is beginning to become more clear and the physical state is taking a background seat, then they start to have time to consider perhaps what they are going home to, the problems that they've got and the situation that they are in at the time. At that particular stage when the physical state has improved a bit, that is a vulnerable time.

Once they have got over the physical aspect of withdrawal, they might be in a position to have a better insight into the problems which affect their lives. They might have a better understanding of the extent of the problems they face. They might feel depressed about these problems. I have been asked whether this clearer insight into their predicament and the hopelessness might in itself give rise to suicidal ideation and I believe that is a possibility. When they've been in the prison for say a period of around three weeks, they are beginning to feel better, they are beginning to eat, perhaps eat a little more and beginning to generally feel better at that stage. It wouldn't happen at the same time for everybody. From what I've seen they begin to pick up physically around the three week period. Some may feel better sooner, but I doubt it, perhaps longer than that.[71]

PRISON MEDICAL OFFICER

It was my feeling that people were vulnerable coming off drugs, perhaps at two or three weeks, perhaps even sooner, and there was some information at that time that most of the suicides occurred, 60 per cent, all within the first week of actual incarceration. So I tended to want to see the prisoners at a week, then a fortnight and then at any time if the block staff were worried about them.[72]

GOVERNOR

Our view of the care of remand prisoners has changed. There is no scientific means of knowing or anticipating which woman is likely to take her life. We all know that there are a number of likely predisposing factors. These predisposing factors, in fact, apply to a lot of women who come into remand, so what we decided to do was apart from those on the prevention of suicide strategy we could treat all the women in remand as potentially vulnerable or not likely to cope with their sentence, which is why we introduced the practice of general observation, simply because it is so difficult to try to determine one from the next, or the most from the least vulnerable.[73]

CLINICAL PSYCHIATRY

The most common method by which people kill themselves in prison is by hanging?

Yes.[74]

CONSULTANT PATHOLOGIST

Can you explain to us please, doctor, how hanging actually causes death?

Well, by compression of major blood vessels that take oxygenated blood to the brain, causing initially anoxia which is a lack of oxygen to the brain, which first renders the person unconscious, and within a minute or two death then supervenes.

Would that be a minute or two from the time that the weight was actually placed on the ligature causing the compression?

Yes.

So the immediate effect of the compression by the ligature is a starvation of oxygen to the brain, is that right?

That's correct.

And does that in turn stop operating in a way that is necessary in order to sustain life?

That's correct.

Can you give us an indication of which life functions close down, as it were, as a result of starvation of oxygen to the brain?

Well, initially, most reflexes are diminished or reduced or nullify totally, and the unconsciousness supervenes, and gradually it becomes irreversible. If it is reversible, you then have certain aspects of the brain that are totally deprived of oxygen. These are non-functionable and therefore, very often, if they are revived, you get ischaemic brain damage in which the person may be able to sustain certain functions, but nevertheless is not the same person ever again.

How long would it take for the person to become unconscious once the ligature had been applied?

Well, unconsciousness can take anything from thirty seconds to a minute. Or even quicker.

Could it be longer?

Yes.

How much longer? What would be the maximum period?

Well, anybody who has sustained stricture of the neck for more than a minute is in serious trouble.

In terms of death, you said it was a minute or two minutes from the pressure being applied?

That's right.

And that would include the time that the person is unconscious?

Yes.

So the whole time from compression to death is one to two minutes?

Yes.

And could it be longer than two minutes or is two minutes the maximum that a person could survive?

Even two minutes is a generous amount, I think.

Before a person loses consciousness, would they lose the ability to help themselves before they actually lose consciousness?

Yes.

And does that mean that if someone applies a ligature to their own neck, takes the weight, that really in a matter of a very few seconds, perhaps five, eight, they will be unable, unless someone comes to help them?

Yes.

Would it be necessary in order to effect death by hanging that the ligature be put at a height above the height of the person or not?

No, it's not necessary at all.

Could death by means of a ligature be effected by a person putting the ligature on something such as the end of a radiator, or a door handle, or the hinge of a door...?

Well, yes, anything actually that will be useful to hold one end of the ligature so that there is pressure around the blood vessels round the neck is sufficient, initially to lose consciousness, and once you've lost consciousness and the body loses its tones so to speak and collapses, further pressure is put on the blood vessels and you reach a stage where it is irreversible.[75]

CLINICAL PSYCHOLOGIST

Hanging as a method of suicide, is that probably the most successful method of suicide in that once you've started to hang yourself you are committed to that and unless there is some other intervention from someone who is going to save you, you can't actually stop once you've started, would that be a fair representation?

Yes, hanging has a low perceived medical fatality but in actual fact it's a high actual medical fatality. It's tragic. Some individuals without suicide intent wish to, for whatever reason, convey the impression of committing suicide but they hang themselves and then seek to right themselves and be discovered but their ability to right themselves is affected by the compression of nerves so there are certainly quite a number of deaths by hanging which were lacking in lethal intent.

But are you in a position to say in most cases of successful suicide, well I don't really think he meant to kill himself or she meant to kill herself.

I think it's a very difficult area except that I'm aware of certain examples such as those engaged in sexual asphyxiation.

The point I was trying to make was that hanging probably is the most successful means of suicide?

It certainly is.

And it is the most common one in prison?

It is.

And perhaps the reason why it is most successful is because there is, once you have started to hang yourself, there's not really much scope for you changing your mind?

No.

There is a possibility in most of the other ways of killing oneself that one could change one's mind and do something about it?

Oh yes.

When you have compressed your airways, you can't physically then stop the asphyxiation?

It varies according to the drop and degree to which the noose is tightened and also the position of the knot where it applies to the nerve on the neck, but yes it can happen on many occasions.[76]

INMATE (18 YEARS OLD)

When you say mental symptoms, what do you mean?

If you're withdrawing from drugs, it can sometimes drive

you to suicide, you can think about suicide and everything. ... It usually happens when you are in your cell and it can sometimes last for weeks.[77]

INMATE (26 YEARS OLD)

It's just, on remand. We're locked up a lot in remand, which means you've got a lot of time to think and too much thinking on your own can be bad for you, because if you are coming off of drugs you are thinking about what you've put your family through, if you've got kids, what you've put your kids through, and you feel really, really low, you've no' got much self confidence. If you are in with someone else at least you can sit and talk your problems over with each other. They've made some improvements in Cornton Vale, they've moved the bars frae the remand block to the outside of the windows instead of the inside. It was suggested a long time ago, I suggested it to the Governor, well, no' the Governor that we've got now, it was a previous Governor. And I told him that the bars should be moved and I was told it would cost too much money but it's been costing all these lives before they've decided to put the bars outside the windows. There might be other ways but the first thing you see is a set of bars when you open the door, so if you have got that in your head then that's the first thing you're gonnae do.[78]

GOVERNOR

Tell me, Cornton Vale was built in the '70s?

1975, my Lord.

Was it kind of regarded as state of the art when it was completed?

Absolutely.

And did it at that stage have the bars inside the cell?

Yes, my Lord.

Had any thought been given to the positioning of the bars inside or outside?

I couldn't say but I think not, because women in prison certainly didn't have a history of suicide.

Are you familiar with the theory that the bars were placed on the inside to make the outside of the prison more attractive and that was the reason why, unusually in prisons, the bars were put on the inside?

No, I haven't heard that, no.[79]

INMATE (26 YEARS OLD)

You said they have not been allowing people to sit in their cells because of what's been going on at Cornton Vale. What did you mean when you said that?

They prefer everybody to sit in the one area, so that they can keep an eye on everybody.

And is that in the sitting area at the back where there is TV and other facilities?

Uh huh.

And for how long have they been encouraging prisoners to go to the sitting room?

They've encouraged it a lot, but a lot more since the suicides have started, but now they lock the doors so that nobody got the opportunity to go into the room and do any harm to themselves.

Do you remember when they started locking the doors?

Frae the suicides started.

Were the cell doors left unlocked before that?

Aye.

When you are in the sitting room, is there an officer with you at that point in time?

No, well, sometimes there would be an officer present, but they feel as if they are babysitting, so they mainly sit in the office so that they are nearby if you need them.

And if someone is known to be sitting in their cell by themselves, what does a prisoner officer do?

Ask them to leave and go up and join the others.[80]

SAMARITANS

The inmates who seek out the services offered by the Samaritans within the prison would appear to have some kind of insight into their own problems to the extent that they have agreed to see a listener?

That's correct.

How many inmates would make use of the service offered by the Samaritans?

Probably one would see during a visit of two hours about five to six people, and possibly only one might be a meaningful contact.

What do you mean by a meaningful contact?

Somebody who is feeling suicidal.

What other reasons might inmates have for seeing the Samaritans?

Lonely, unhappy, isolated, fearful.

Can you tell us generally what the listener scheme is?

It's training prisoners who have been selected by the Samaritans to become similar to Samaritans within the prison setting.

So it is one inmate speaking to another?

That is correct.

Are rules about confidentiality imposed?

Absolutely.

There is no question of an inmate who is participating in the listener scheme going off to tell the prison authorities things that another inmate has told them without their permission?

No.

When did the listener scheme begin to operate?

July was the starting date of the training and it takes six to eight weeks, so I think it was October when five listeners were trained.

Have you any idea of how many inmates have actually gone along to see listeners?

On average it is about five a week, just under one per day.[81]

PROFESSOR OF PSYCHIATRY

It may well be that people who are in the vulnerable category we are talking about have had adverse experiences at an earlier stage of their life. That kind of theory would need to be tested out in a scientific way. I have no data, but if I were doing experiments I would look for rejection experiences, or some sort of childhood adverse factor which makes them more vulnerable to feel that life is not for them in their adulthood. One of the things that I did when I first started psychiatry was to look at the childhood experiences of people who had made suicide attempts in the hospital, and experience of loss, experiences of separation in breaking from their parents in a particular way in their childhood occurred more commonly in the group that attempted suicide than in other patients. There's an increasing amount of information about these predisposing factors in childhood which are important but the science needs to be done.[82]

PRISON OFFICER

Have there been, during your period as a prison officer, occasions when people have attempted to take their own life, and either you or some of your colleagues have managed to stop them?

Yes.

And has that been almost, if you like, in the middle of the act?

Well, yes. A couple of them have actually stopped breathing and had to be resuscitated. On one occasion it was the gurgling that had been heard, and it was a prisoner actually heard this girl and alerted the staff, and we were lucky enough that the two staff got there in time and were able to revive the girl, yes.

So does that mean that if you're a prison officer, you may expect in the course of your career to find someone in the act of trying to take their own life?

I wouldn't say that, no, it was never an expectation I had when I joined the service.

But in the light of experience, have you discovered that that's so?

Yes.[83]

PRISON SUPERVISOR

The staff morale in the remand block has been very difficult to assess over the past 18 to 20 months because of the suicides we've had in the block. It's been very, very difficult for the staff and it's been trying and, it's difficult to explain, it's not what would be the norm for working in the residential areas. It was just different, the atmosphere was different. The staff all pulled together and were very, very supportive to one another and to the prisoners. It's just been a strange atmosphere in there. There's been a lot of changes within the prison. Everything that happens in Cornton Vale obviously has a knock effect to all those who are within but the biggest thing to us was certainly the suicides.[84]

MEDICAL PROFESSOR

If there is a suicide at a prison, do you expect that there is an increased risk of another one?

I think there is sufficient evidence of clustering to indicate that the awareness of staff needs to be heightened even more in a period after a suicide.

Do you know why that should be?

Absolutely no idea. I mean there are lots of guesses but they are just guesses.

In laymen's terms, everybody is very upset by a suicide and so there is a risk that someone who is upset anyway will become more upset and they might follow suit? Could that be one of the layman's ways of looking at it?

Well, it could be. I mean there is no scientific basis for being able to say there will be a cluster and how big it will be and what will happen, but there is enough anecdotal evidence of clustering to make people conscious and aware of the fact that things can happen subsequently and the levels of distress after a suicide within the service amongst staff and amongst inmates is very significant.[85]

FORMER PRISON MEDICAL OFFICER

By the time we are speaking of, there had been five suicides in recent times in the prison. Would it be a bit of a topic of conversation?

I think it is. It especially worries people who have never been in a prison before. It very much worries a first offender, not knowing what they are coming into and all they have heard about is the suicides.[86]

PRISON CHAPLAIN

It's not an uncommon thing for some girls to talk about previous suicides in the prison, and the suicides were for a time the topic of conversation in the remand block, and it wasn't unusual for girls to say, 'I'm going to be next, I'm going to be next.'[87]

INMATE (17 YEARS OLD)

Did you become friendly with Denise Devine when she was in Unit 4?

The night before she done that tae herself, aye a wis talkin' tae her that night.

And can you tell us where you spoke to her that evening?

In the sitting room an' she got ginger tae gie aw the lassies some. Ah went intae her room wi her, ah took some o' her ginger an' we wur jist talkin' away tae her.

What sort of mood was Denise in that evening?

Ah wis carryin' on wae her, ah'm always the clown on the unit, always carryin' on.

Do I take it from that that she was in quite a good mood?

Aye.

Were you having a laugh?

Aye. She wis also comin' aff methadone as well. She said she didnae take heroin an' aw that, jist methadone an' pills, she took pills. She wis pure ill. Strung out for methadone. Ye cannae eat, ye cannae be bothered, ye're jist sick aw the time. Ah wis in her room an' ah ran oot it 'cause somebody had previously hung theirsel' in that room before, an' a ran oot it. She went 'why're ye daen this?' Ah says, ah don't like it in there, ah jist remembered somebody hung theirsel' in there.[88]

INMATE (17 YEARS OLD)

Do you remember an occasion when Angela might have been joking about hurting herself?

Aye, it was a couple of days before she died.

And can you tell us where the incident took place?

It was in the sitting room. There were a few other lassies there.

And what did Angela do?

Because people had done it before, she was just joking about it. She was just saying 'imagine' and she put the curtain round her neck and she was carrying on.

Had that happened before, other girls joking about previous hanging incidents?

Some people, aye.

Do inmates talk about previous hangings from time to time?

Yes.

And then there would be these black jokes about it, is that right?

Just the odd person.

Not every inmate would think this was something to make a joke about?

Well, most of them thought it was quite sick.

And when this joke was made, what would be the reaction of most of the inmates?

Some of them would laugh and other ones wouldn't think it was funny at all.

Would it be unusual for someone to make a joke like that?

No' really, because we were talking about it before she done it, before she made the joke.

And were all the inmates from the unit in the sitting room with you when this discussion was taking place?

I cannae really remember.

I'm trying to get a picture of what was going on at the time. I mean, it's not the situation that you were all sitting around in a big semi-circle with all the other people and all sharing your views on the matter, is it?

We were just talking about suicides in Cornton Vale, and wondering how they done it, wondering how they committed suicide.

I take it this would be a very serious discussion?

No' really, we were just, well, we had nothing else to talk about so we were just talking about suicides.[89]

PRISON OFFICER

We've heard that within the prison sitting room, inmates have joked about hanging. Now, while it seems shocking in the context of this Court, that wouldn't particularly shock you, would it?

The girls will do it as shock tactics now, and they will use it as a means of blackmail. Personally, a prisoner has approached me and said they wanted something, and I've said no, that's not happening, and they've went 'Give me it, or else I will hang myself. You can't afford another hanging in here, and that's what I'll do' and it's awful, it's horrible.[90]

INMATE (18 YEARS OLD)

Can you tell us why you think that joking about suicide is a matter for concern?

Because there's a lot of people, you ken, in Cornton Vale you can tell they are suicidal.

How is it you can tell that?

Because I used to be like that myself. Before I came into jail, when I was outside.

And when you say 'like that', do you mean suicidal?

Yes. I know how it feels. I've tried to commit suicide quite a few times.[91]

INMATE (27 YEARS OLD)

And then after she was found dead, I heard that she'd asked

another girl before how to make a noose. I think they were talking about a previous hanging and she sort of said it casually, 'Oh, how do you make a noose anyway?' [92]

INMATE (34 YEARS OLD)

I was sitting in the Unit sitting room talking to Denise. I forget what our conversation was all about, but at one point Denise asked me how to make a noose. I was quite taken aback and I said to her, 'What do you want to know a thing like that for? You wouldn't do a thing like that, would you?' And she said 'No, I couldnae.' She said, 'Hey, don't tell them I said that, because I was only kidding on.'

She had heard the lassies saying earlier on when we were talking about it, the other lassies that were depressed an' that, and they said you get put in the back if you are depressed and maybe that's how. I'm no' sayin' that was why she wasnae wanting to tell them, but after she died I said that's maybe why she wasnae wanting to say anything. She wouldnae want to get put down the back, in the strict sui'.

Strict suicide supervision?

Aye.

Did the inmates in the block know what strict suicide supervision involved?

Aye.

And was it unpopular with the inmates?

Aye.

What was it people didn't like about the idea?

Because they take your clothes off you and that and your belongings. You don't get much, no mirrors or that and no sinks. Just a bare cell.

You had told the officers about suicidal talk before?

I know I told them about one wee girl that I was concerned about. She was only 17 and she got put on strict suicide, and she didnae like it.

What had she been talking about, do you remember?

Well, I found a noose below her mattress.[93]

FORMER PRISON MEDICAL OFFICER

If you do make a decision that an inmate is imminently at risk of committing suicide, does it have the consequence that she will be put on what is called Triple S, strict suicide supervision?

That's correct.

That's a particular regime within the prison which is intended, if I understand it correctly, to prevent people from killing themselves because they won't have the means to do it?

That's correct.

Is it a regime which could have it's own harmful effects?

Very much so.

So it is something you apply with care and caution?

Absolutely.

I suppose some people might say that an easy way for a doctor in the prison service would be to put a whole lot of people onto that regime and that way the doctor will, if you'll forgive me, cover his own back?

That's correct.

Now what would you think of that as a professional way of proceeding, would that be right?

No, it wouldn't and it wouldn't be helpful to the patient you are dealing with. The strict suicide supervision, as you know, is really a very restricted regime. It's the stripped cells, particularly of clothing, there's a fair degree of social deprivation and if somebody who's depressed but not suicidal, probably the worst thing you could do for them is to put them into an area where their depression is going to worsen because of the social deprivation and all the rest of it. If they are depressed but not deemed suicidal, then they need support. They need to be in a unit where they've got support from other inmates that may help, support from officers that they may know from the past, but at least on a regime where they're not isolated. Triple S is perceived as a punishment by some prisoners.[94]

INMATE (16 YEARS OLD)

I was put in a Triple S cell with three other girls. There were four mattresses on the ground and four sleeping bags with a couple of bedpans and plastic cups to get a drink from. We got to mix with the other inmates during the day but when we were in there, we were only allowed to wear black shorts and tee-shirts and had to leave everything else outside, including cigarettes and that sort of stuff. We had to strip in front of one another and two female prison warders every time we were going in or out of the cell. This could be several times a day.

We were wakened about 6.30am for tea and toast and we had to get changed and go and get the tea and toast. About 8 o'clock we had to get changed back into the shorts and tee-shirts and were back in the cell until 10.30am when we were allowed out with the other inmates.

If they were short-staffed, however, we were put back onto the Triple S cells for dinner and got out again after it. That would be us until bed-time at 9.30pm when we got into the black tee-shirts and shorts into the cell. They checked on us every 15 minutes in the cell, just coming in and waking us up and making sure we were OK but the rest of the time when we were out and about we were just like the rest of the prisoners.

If anything, I think the Triple S cell made me even more depressed, having to strip in front of people all the time and being stuck in there with 3 other people. One of the lassies I was in with is now in Carstairs. She tried to commit suicide just about every single day. One night she set her hair on fire when she slipped a lighter into the cell and another time when the screws came in to check on us, she was blue in the face trying to strangle herself with her tee-shirt underneath the sleeping bag.[95]

INMATE (19 YEARS OLD)

After Angela hung hersel', ah smashed up ma cell. Ah wis put on Triple S. It jist made me feel worse. They're jist coverin' their ain backsides in case ye dae it. Ah didnae feel suicidal before Triple S but it made me suicidal.[96]

PRISON SUPERVISOR

In my opinion someone that's put behind their door to cool off, that's no going to make them kill themselves. It's no' as if they're completely isolated, there's other prisoners going up and down the corridors, they do shout in to them, they do stand at the doors and talk to them. If you've got umpteen prisoners to look after, you can't always keep them away, so that they do have constant contact. But there are occasions when they're all on their own, their doors shut, but it doesnae mean they're gonna kill themselves.[97]

INMATE (19 YEARS OLD)

You heard Mr Thompson shout 'help'?

That's when ah wis in the sittin' room, that's how ah came oot, aw the commotion.

And so when you came out, he was at the door of cell 6, was he?

Aye, he wis gawn in partly jist as ah approached, ah'd been lookin' doon an' when ah looked back up, he wis in the room. The pie and beans was aw o'er the wa' an' the flairs an' aw that.

Where did you go at that stage?

Ah wis runnin' doon tae ma room tae see whit wis wrang. It wis ma room he wis in.

And can you tell us what happened then?

Another officer took me back tae the sittin' room. Ah don't know who it wis, cannae mind anythin' efter that.

How long did you stay in the living room after being taken back there?

Well, we always haud a tea party if there's a death, right, a karaoke an' aw that.[98]

INMATE (17 YEARS OLD)

I got this poem while I was in Cornton Vale. It was a poem that was passed round all the prisoners and some of us had a copy.

The jailbird wrote home one day
To find her true love gone away.
When she wrote to find out why
This was the boy's reply:
If you had led an honest life
You could gladly be my wife
But since you chose a life of crime
Jailbird, go do your time.

The jailbird did ring her bell
All the screws ran to her cell
They found her dead
With this note upon her bed:
Dig my grave and dig it deep
Put red roses round my feet
On my chest a turtle dove
To show the world I died of love.

So they dug her grave and dug it deep
Put red roses round her feet
On her chest a turtle dove
To show the world she died of love
So all you boys bear in mind
A jailbird is hard to find
But if you find one, love her true
'Cause that jailbird would die for you.[99]

PRISON SUPERVISOR

We will never know, you will never ever be able to quantify the amount of people that you have stopped actually going to attempt to take their own life, by whatever action or deed that you've done at that time. It's just one of those things that we will never, ever know.[100]

PART FOUR

Yvonne in Prison

CHAPTER 14

Cornton Vale, December 1996

CAROLANN

Yvonne had been in Cornton Vale a few times, but only for minor offences. She never sent out any visitor's passes because she didn't want to see us in prison. We never went to see her in prison. She would never let us. We used to always say to her that no matter what if she wanted us to go and visit her we would go and visit her but she never sent us any passes.

She used to phone us from prison, usually for us to send money in. She never seemed down or depressed and was never in for long. Once she did say there was a girl in prison who thought she was a 'hard ticket' – that was the phrase she used. She felt she was going to get picked on by this girl. I told her to stay out of trouble.

PRISON SOCIAL WORKER

On the 4th September 1996 I was on social work duty at the prison when I got a call from a social worker in Glasgow to tell me that Yvonne Gilmour was coming in to the prison, that she wanted to be sentenced, she was quite happy to receive a sentence and that he had information that she had been parasuicidal in the past.

I completed an internal memo with this information to be added to her files.[101]

MICHELLE

The day after Yvonne got remanded at Cornton Vale in December I got a phone call from her. She told me where she was and that she was remanded until the 23rd of December. I asked where she had been lifted from and she told me 'The hostel.' I think it was the YMCA but I wasn't sure. She sounded alright, a bit down but not crying or anything.

We later heard from her girlfriend Linda that after Red

Tower Yvonne had gone to stay in the hostel where Linda was. Yvonne was depressed because Linda was coping coming off smack and Yvonne was struggling. Linda said they got on well and could talk to each other because they had suffered similar upsets in the past. They came from the same kind of backgrounds, she said.

One day at the beginning of December Yvonne took a hit and Linda got upset and dumped the works that Yvonne had somehow got hold of. That was a few days before she got lifted. Linda said that was why Yvonne was arrested, because she was struggling coming off smack. She had got hold of a bottle of vodka and drunk it. She reacts badly to drink. She started a fight with another resident and Linda couldn't calm her down. Yvonne said she needed something from the doctor so she called the doctor and she came about one in the morning. Yvonne was really upset apparently. Anyway she got lifted that night.

PRISON CHAPLAIN

On the 10th December I was with the other chaplain in an office where we could meet inmates privately who were newly admitted. Yvonne was the last of about four or five inmates that afternoon. I had never met her before but the other chaplain had. Yvonne seemed quite sad that day. She talked about a lot of her problems with us. In particular she talked about her drug habit, which she said she was trying to come to terms with. It was our understanding that she was trying to give it up. She talked about the loss of her partner in the summertime, and she talked about some problems that dated back to her earlier life. She spoke about early sexual abuse, and about disclosing her own sexual orientation to her family, about being put out of home, about being in trouble as a youngster and about beginning a drugs habit from an early teenage year. She was very upset during the interview. She was weeping, particularly in connection with the sexual abuse she spoke about.

She gave me the impression, and I'm almost certain she said so, that she was glad to be in prison. She felt that given the time in prison, she would take the opportunity to try and deal with some of her problems. She also said she was glad about being in prison because of the drugs habit and the effect drugs were having on her. She felt she was quite capable of doing something drastic to a partner, or to someone, because she had a lot of anger and rage inside her. She said she was capable of an act of violence against someone. She felt more protected in the prison. She spoke about suicides in the prison and she said that she could do something to herself also in prison if she didn't get her act together, in the vein of 'I'm going to do something if I don't get my act together, don't get my head together.'

The interview came to an end because the women were about to be served their evening meal. Yvonne said she needed some toiletries and that she didn't feel well in herself, and that being able to have access to toiletries, she would feel better. So we agreed to get those for her.

We expressed our concern about Yvonne to one of the officers and we recorded the following note in her file:

Spoke confidentially to us about family history. Is aware of how deep rooted her problems are. Spoke of recent bereavement regarding her partner. No family visits. Seems to us vulnerable at the moment.[102]

PRISON CHAPLAIN

I had already met Yvonne in prison in July. It was towards the end of her stay and she was quite hopeful that she was going to do well when she went out. When I saw her on the 10th December, along with the other prison chaplain, I recognised her and she recognised me, so we got into conversation quite freely. She was a totally changed girl, that's what struck me, she was so different from the woman I had met in July. She was sad, she was a broken type of person. I think she realised what she had been doing to herself in the course of speaking. It wasn't an investigative interview. In my role as a pastor, I see myself as a pastoral care worker and my job is to listen, so I wouldn't have interrupted her and asked her any questions. She proceeded to tell me whatever she wanted to say.

She said she hoped to get sentenced so that it would give her a chance to get her life together.

She seemed a little cheered up at the end of the interview. She talked about toiletries and the very fact that she was concerned about her appearance I think meant that she was a little bit cheered up at the end.

We worded our report carefully. We knew that if we wrote 'seems a bit vulnerable at the moment' that certain other services would be seeing her, psychological and medical services would be taking care of her.[103]

YVONNE

Form no. 259
Untried Prisoner's Letter

NOTICE CONCERNING COMMUNICATIONS WITH PRISONERS

All letters are read by the Authorities, who may keep them back if they think it is right to do so. Every letter will be kept back in the following cases:

If it is not written so as to be easily read
If it is not expressed in proper and temperate language
No unpaid letters will be received into the Prison.

H.M.Institution
Cornton Road
Stirling

Name: *Yvonne Gilmour*
Hall: *Romeo*

Tuesday night

Dear Linda,

I really don't know where to start. My head's done right in but after Saturday night when I got lifted I think you seen that? I'm really sorry, babes. I was looking for you in the Court, I didn't even see Paula till she came down the cells which was nice of her. So will you thank her for me. I know you wasn't in the Court room but I know you would of been there for me. I ain't gonna lie to you but when I go back up Court on the 23rd Dec

I'm gonna get six months. I was crazy in the Court so I don't think I'll get a back dater. Linda, I really do love you. I know you don't believe me but please give me a chance to get my head together, come off all the shit. It's gonna be hard but I'll swear I'll do it for you. That's if you still want me? Well I don't know anyone in here so you don't have to worry about anything. I'll be thinking of my No.1 girl!

I'm gonna start getting help next week, try and talk about my past which is gonna be hard cos I really can't handle it but I'll get there. I should be the strongest one out of us but babes you beat me hands down. I don't know how you do it. You're the best.

Well, I feel like fucking shit so please try and come and see me and bring some up for a girl called Maggie, alright? She'll be wearing my silk shirt that I had on at Court and the waist coat, and she knows it will be big Dave, alright babes? But if you can't get anyone it don't really matter as long as I can see you. But it would help if he could come if you know what I mean!!! (help me please someone, somewhere out there)

Paula had me in tears. I told her to tell you that 'I loved you' and always will, and she told me you love me too so that started me off. I should of got this out to you today Tuesday but my head was done in last night and I just could not get it together. But you should get it before Friday. Fuck knows what I'm gonna do. I ain't even got a smoke, still maybe I could stop, hey, I don't think so! Smoking more like Choking! I need you babes as in yesterday, just hang in there please for me, god you're all I've got in the world apart from my sisters. Did you ring them and let them know. I need some telephone numbers. Send me up the phone book plus ring Paula for me, alright babes? Thanks.

Well, it's almost six o'clock so we will be getting out soon I hope. I know I ain't gonna get a visit tonight but I wish I was cos I need to see my baby. Fucking hell, when will I touch, hold you in my arms, kiss your lips???????? 1997 some time.... I'll write more later as that's us getting out, don't go away cos I'll be back. That's me back. I could hear keys but we're still locked up. Story of my life at the moment.

I almost died when I seen the police. That was that Doctor, fucking slag. I should of killed her, still she never charged me so that was alright of her. Hey Linda! I just lost it Saturday night, can't even remember much about it. I woke up in Govan Cop Shop with my head right up my arse. Thats the drink for you, I'll never touch it again. Well, I'm gonna love you and leave you for now but I'll be back. Well, it's 8.15p.m. and we are still locked up. It's a fucking joke, hey.

Hello, it's me again on the bill and ben with a few lines before I get my head down. Linda, they say 'You always hurt the one you love' and I'm so sorry, please believe me, but I'll understand if you don't. When I get out, things will be different I promise, no more drugs or drink for that matter, that just sends me crazy plus all them pills. The turnkey said on Sunday morning they couldn't get me awake, god knows how I didn't OD. *Well I'm still here, so that's all that matters apart from being in jail.*

Babes ring Paula and ask her to give you something for me. She will, even bring her up on a visit. By the way, they are looking in everyone's mouths before they let them in so just let Dave know.

I'm gonna write to my cousin in Bar and get something done to your brother or should I say so-called brother, anyway fuck him or he will be getting fucked. I was going to ring you tonight but I forgot the number, I swear my head's away with the birds. Anyway, I'm gonna get my head down so please write soon, if not sooner.

I love you, Linda,
With all my heart and soul
Step by step
Day by Day
Missing you all the way
All my love,
Gilly G. That's me.[104]

CHAPTER 15

Fellow Inmates

INMATE (19 YEARS OLD)

Yvonne had a Scottish and English accent, a bit of a mixture. Scouser we called her. She wis a crackin' girl. Everyone got on wi' her.[105]

INMATE (19 YEARS OLD)

I first met Yvonne when she was brought in for sentence in summer 1996. It was in the kitchens. I think it was just the first day she had come in. She shouted at me that she was going to kill me because of the crime I had been convicted of committing, but I just ignored her. Yvonne started off by saying that but then she started talking to me and explained that she had said that because of my case being on television, so we started to get on after that. At that time Yvonne was going out with a girl I know, and later they both came up to my unit and we just sat talking. After that we became the best of friends and got on really well together. I think it was because I stood up to her and that's how we became such good friends.

Yvonne was only in for about a month at the most, then she was liberated and went to a rehab place. She still kept in touch, wrote to me and phoned me now and again and I used to phone her.

She was in again for another short sentence a bit later and we got on well then too. She was always the type of happy-go-lucky girl and used to stick up for me if anyone gave me a hassle. She didn't get into fights or anything like that but she would always argue her case and stick up for me.

She was always a brilliant laugh. She used to talk to me with the rest of the girls but didn't say much about her family or anything like that, just talked in general about things we were having a carry on with.

When she was released she went to a drug rehab centre in Helensburgh. She wrote to me once from there. She didn't seem too happy there and said they could only get one phone call a week. The next thing I knew she was back in Cornton Vale.[106]

INMATE (33 YEARS OLD)

Initially I didn't like Yvonne. I thought she was extremely cocky and I didn't have much to do with her. I hardly ever spoke to her and kept out of her way. Then I met her again during the summer of 1996 and I got to know her better and thought she was OK. We were in different units but we used to see quite a lot of each other. She was always a cheery, happy-go-lucky character and she never seemed to have any problems within the prison.

INMATE (24 YEARS OLD)

I first met Yvonne when I arrived in prison in December. I met her on remand. She was a very bubbly person and she was also very talkative We were in different units but she used to come down to my room a lot. When I say a lot, I mean at least once a day, but I never went up to her room except for one time, I think. I don't know why that was. It just happened like that. We used to meet up a lot in the sitting room in my unit as well. She told me she had been in prison before. She also told me she was gay and she told me about her girlfriends in and out of prison.

I don't know if Yvonne was a drug user or not although she did tell me she liked taking drugs, usually smack or hash, but she liked to try a bit of anything. I don't know if she was getting any drugs while she was in prison but I suppose if she was she would have told me about it because, as I said, we were quite friendly and she probably told me everything that happened to her while she was in prison.

I know that Yvonne was on medication in Cornton Vale because a couple of times she kept her DFs for me as I was coming down off drugs myself and it was making me ill. She did that about three or four times.

There was another girl in our unit, I don't remember her name, and Yvonne had given her a pair of trainers and in turn this girl was giving Yvonne her DFs. It happened quite a few times. The other girl got caught and had to go up in front of the governor because of it.

Yvonne was also getting valium at medication but she wasn't getting any extra because it was crushed and you had to take it in front of the nurses and prison officers. You had to take the DFs in front of them as well but it was easy to hide them in your mouth because the prison officers didn't search you properly and some were even less strict than others.

We were given four DFs a day, two in the morning and two at night and sometimes Yvonne was managing to get a double dose. If you get enough of these, they could give you a high and if Yvonne was taking eight, it would have been enough to give her a buzz.

INMATE (38 YEARS OLD)

I've been in Cornton Vale a few times but always as a remand prisoner. I've never been sentenced.

I met Yvonne in remand in December. I spoke to her if not every day then most days when we were watching TV or just milling about chatting to one another. She always struck me as a happy bright girl who got on well with just about everyone and never found herself in any problems. She was never aggressive or pushy. She was more like laughing and geeing people along.

Everybody in the prison has their low points when you get a bit depressed and feel down. I don't suppose Yvonne was any different from the rest of us and there must have been times when she didn't feel too great, like when she was due to go to Court, she was a bit down. But she always came round quickly and was always trying to gee other people up if they were upset or down.

I know she was a lesbian but I never knew her to have any problems in this respect, either from fellow prisoners or members of staff. She was quite open about being a lesbian but she wasn't pushy about it and at the same time she wasn't trying to hide it. When I met her, I actually put my foot in it. I asked her if she had any children and when she said no, I asked her why not. She just laughed and told me she was gay and it was women she went with and that she didn't go with men. I was a bit flustered because I thought I had put my foot in it but she took it in good part and just joked about it.

INMATE (29 YEARS OLD)

I always found Yvonne to be a dead cheery person, always outgoing and full of fun. The only thing she complained about was not being allowed to see her girlfriend. That really did her nut in. She used to keep going down the back cells to try and see her but she was always getting caught and that really pissed her off. She had no problems with the staff other than that. She seemed to get on with just about everyone. And I'm sure she wasn't having any problems with any of the prisoners because Yvonne could look after herself. In fact, I remember on one occasion she heard that somebody in another unit had said they were going to do her for something or another, I don't know what. Anyway, Yvonne goes up to the unit sitting room where all the girls from that unit were sitting watching telly, and she turned the television off and stood there and asked who it was that wanted to do her. She never got any response because it was quite obvious she could look after herself.

INMATE (19 YEARS OLD)

How long did you share a cell with Yvonne Gilmour?

About two weeks.

Did she have anything to complain about in particular when you shared a cell with her?

She says that the staff were givin' her a hassle because of her being a lesbian. She told me that they kept calling her it, saying snide remarks to her.

Presumably they weren't calling her 'it', they must have been calling her a name?

She says that two male staff members were slagging her, saying she was a lesbian and giving her a hard time.

Did she say what words were used?

The exact words Yvonne gave me was 'dykie bastard'.

Were you shocked at that?

Yes.

I mean, there's no need for that, is there?

I didn't think the staff would say something like that.

So you were shocked?

Yes.[107]

INMATE (23 YEARS OLD)

I first met Yvonne years ago outside the prison. I palled about with her and the two of us used to go shoplifting together round various shops in Glasgow. She was a happy-go-lucky person, to me anyway, and I was very close to her. I actually spent two or three nights in that hostel with her. I've always known that Yvonne was a lesbian but I'm not. When I met her in prison in the middle of December it was in the medical room. I was getting painkillers for my headache. Yvonne gave me a cuddle and asked me why I was back in prison. I had only been released in September after serving a 15-month sentence. I saw her quite a lot after that when we visited each other in the prison. I never saw her down in the dumps. She seemed quite happy really with no complaints.[108]

INMATE (30 YEARS OLD)

I got to know Yvonne because on the night she was remanded she was brought in with my sister-in-law's young sister and they were two'd up together for a night or two. I remember the first night I met Yvonne she asked me for drink of lemonade and I gave her a cup of my Irn Bru. She didn't actually tell me that she was a lesbian but I knew almost straight away because she was dressed in jeans, a checked shirt and a waistcoat. I come from the Govan area of Glasgow where there are a lot of gay girls and they all dress very similar to that, in a sort of mannish fashion.

I didn't speak much to Yvonne on the first day but on the next day I did and that's when I realised she had quite a sense of humour.

I remember she actually came looking for me and when she found me she said, 'Are you the lassie that gave me the juice last night?' and when I said I was she said, 'God, I thought you were a fucking guy.' That's the type of person she was, quite comical.

Yvonne came across as a really nice lassie, very happy-go-lucky but she could get a bit down at times and would start crying, that sort of thing. Any time she was down, I used to ask her what was wrong, if she wanted to talk, but she usually said No, just to leave her alone, and when she was on a downer she stayed in her room and wouldn't speak to anyone.

I remember that a couple of days after she came into the prison, I walked into the sitting room and Yvonne was sitting on the back of a chair – a sort of office chair with her feet on the seat. The chair was at the window and Yvonne was staring blankly out of the window. Her head was down as if she was upset. I asked her what was wrong and she said she was pissed off. She just wasn't in the mood for talking. It wasn't that she'd fallen out with anyone. She just used to get these downers now and again and there was no talking to her.

She didn't tell me anything about herself or why she was in prison and I don't know if she abused drugs or not. She didn't look like a drug addict to me as she always kept herself pretty smart and spotless. I've seen lots of other girls in here who abuse drugs on the outside and they don't seem half as bright or particular about their appearance as Yvonne did.

INMATE (18 YEARS OLD)

How was Yvonne Gilmour during the time that you were with her in Glasgow Sheriff Court cells and on the trip to Cornton Vale?

She was just as she usually is.

And what was usual for her?

Awful happy, you know, chirpy and joking, that sort of thing.[109]

CHAPTER 16

Prison Authority

PRISON OFFICER

Did Yvonne seem to be a cheerful girl or not?

Not cheerful.

How would you describe her then?

She was almost quite hyperactive, and some days she was down and some days she was up. She was quite erratic.

Would you say she was anti-authority?

I would with some officers, yes.

What about you, did you get on alright with her?

Yes, I got on fine with her.[110]

PRISON OFFICER

Yvonne Gilmour was fairly happy-go-lucky, her own person, did her own thing. She could be a bit awkward on occasions. There had been problems about sharing. She could be quite a hard girl to get along with. It was hard to find people who were compatible.

I wouldn't say she had a discipline problem as such, but she was very strong-willed and single-minded. She didn't like being told what to do.[111]

PRISON SUPERVISOR

And then we have your comments here where it says she doesn't mind sharing a room, but says she's gay?

That's correct.

Was that something that you knew about Yvonne anyway?

Yes, I did know that about Yvonne but I quoted what she said when I wrote that.

Because you might allocate her to share with someone who might object to sharing with a gay person, so it would be important that was known?

Yes, but it was Yvonne who wanted it known, because she didn't want to be put in a compromising situation where somebody finds out she's gay and they want out of the room and it causes bother. She wanted people to be quite up front about it, know that's how she was and if they accepted to share a room with her, she was quite happy about that.

In your experience were there some girls who objected to sharing with somebody who was gay?

Yes.

Now you said she was very confident and then you've written down an expression 'worth watching as she's very stroppy with the staff'?

That's correct.

Was she stroppy with you?

Not cheeky, but quite strong-willed you could say. She was very adamant about some things when she was talking, like I will share a room but you better make sure that it's no' an old gay, and I don't want to just share with anybody, that type of thing. It was coming across that she could be quite stroppy.

Why did she need to be watched?

Yvonne partly needed to be watched because of the withdrawals and partly because she could be quite strong-willed and if the staff weren't aware of it, they might not be aware of some of the things that she would be up to.

Did you know Yvonne before you filled in this form?

I had previously worked with Yvonne. I knew her as she had been in the block before. I knew the kind of behaviour pattern she had from before and she wasnae, let's say, she wasn't shy and retiring. She was very up front and very challenging and if she thought she was not being treated fairly or wasnae getting what she wanted she wouldn't be long in letting everyone know about it.

You said she needed a firm hand. What did you mean by that?

I meant if she wasnae kept under control she would just do

> what she wanted and very much the message I was getting at the time when I spoke to her. Yvonne could be very, very assertive, she wouldn't always take a telling on discipline matters. Yvonne could get quite out of hand if she wasn't watched and had a firm hand.

Extracts from Prison Observation Form for Yvonne Gilmour

12th December

A pain in the neck. Was told to keep away from the window in the sitting room as she was shouting out to the girls from Bravo Block going to the Health Centre. Was told that if caught at it again, she would find herself on report. Has been fine since.

13th December

Yvonne was caught up in a wrangle re visit with girlfriend, ex-prisoner Linda McGill. Was allowed a closed visit with Linda. Had quite a temper tantrum when initially refused a visit and request now through book.

16th December

Not happy sharing with prisoner Kay Henderson. She was told she would have to wait until we found out how many we were getting in tonight and she was quite happy with that.

20th December

Yvonne was a pain in the neck. She was locked up after dub-up and we reckoned she threw her rice pudding all over the sitting room wall. Someone else took the blame, saying she fell over the table. We let her out about 8.40 to make tea by which time she had calmed down.

If you look at this observation sheet, could it be an example of someone who is not coping with prison, by throwing their dinner at the wall, they're not happy sharing with someone, they're

being a pain in the neck, could that not be an example of somebody who is just not coping?

It could also be an example of somebody who doesn't want to conform or who wants to choose where they want to be housed, pick the room, pick the person they're with, and that's not always possible.[112]

PRISON OFFICER

Can you look at the extract for the 13th of December? Is that your handwriting?

It is.

It says *Yvonne was caught up in a wrangle re visit with girlfriend, ex-prisoner Linda McGill. Was allowed a closed visit with Linda. Had quite a temper tantrum when initially refused a visit and request now through book.* **Could you tell me please the circumstances whereby this wrangle, as you call it, came about?**

Yvonne had asked for a visit with ex-prisoner Linda McGill and she had been wanting a closed visit and she couldn't have a closed visit with this prisoner. She had made the request earlier that day and the early shift officer would have passed it on to me when I came on late shift that Yvonne had made the request and it had not been granted.

Are there rules about visits from ex-prisoners?

Ex-prisoners are not normally encouraged to visit at the prison unless there are special circumstances or close family relationships. Ex-prisoners are not generally allowed in for visits.

And who had been responsible for turning down Yvonne's request?

I believe it would be security.

Now, in what circumstances did you become involved in a wrangle about the visit?

Yvonne was being difficult, she was having a temper tantrum so I went to see why she wasn't going on her visit because she was quite happy to have a closed visit.

Now can I be quite clear about this policy? Is it the rule that ex-prisoners are not allowed any visit at all or is it the rule that ex-prisoners can visit but only on a closed visit system?

No. Any prisoner wishing an ex-prisoner to visit must request it.

So it is a discretionary matter?

No, each person is gone into, their background, whether the person has got drug offences, if the ex-prisoner has brought drugs into prison. There's a whole lot of things come into it, a whole lot of factors. Each case is judged on its own merit.

Yvonne was told that her request had been denied...?

I had been told. I had to tell Yvonne. I think she already knew that her visit had been turned down. She was angry because she had already arranged for the person to come and visit and the person would be arriving. She had gone to all this trouble and why wasn't she being allowed her visit. She was quite happy with a closed visit.

Could you describe for us please the temper tantrum that Yvonne had?

She was just shouting and she went storming off to her room, slammed the door, shouting and screaming and what have you.

What sort of thing was she shouting?

I really don't remember, probably a lot of abuse.

Was it quite an extreme reaction to the situation?

Yvonne could be very volatile. She was angry about the visit. She had gone to a lot of trouble and the person was coming through from wherever to visit and she was getting really agitated and upset.

What did you then do?

I went and told Yvonne that I would go and see what I could do, see what I could find out for her, but she had better calm herself down.

And what was her reaction?

Oh, she was just prepared to wait and see what was going to happen.

And then you...?

From what I can remember I contacted the supervisor to find out why she couldn't have her visit and they couldn't tell me why she couldn't have a closed visit either so eventually it was agreed that she could have a closed visit in this instance.

So no-one could tell you why her request had been refused?

I would assume it was because the ex-prisoner had a previous record for bringing drugs into the prison or something like that untoward. I really don't know. I never made it my business to go and find out. But I was quite annoyed that she couldn't be allowed a closed visit.

Did you think that that was something that was unfair?

Well, I didn't think it was, it wasn't for me to say it was yes or it wasn't but I mean I wanted to understand why she wasn't being allowed a closed visit in this instance.

You have just said that you were annoyed...?

I was annoyed, yes.

Yes?

Well, it was us that was left to deal with all the flak.

Would you agree that visits are something of importance to prisoners?

Oh yes, they are, they are very important.

And if they have made an arrangement for a visit it may be a great disappointment for them if they are told they can't have it?

Very much so.

Presumably that is one of the reasons you went to make some efforts to find out if she could have a visit?

Yes, plus if Yvonne hadn't got a visit I dread to think what kind of state she would have gotten herself into.

And is that in connection with a visit?

Yvonne had requested to have a visit with this ex-prisoner.

And you have recorded that she was allowed a closed visit, is that right?

Yes.

What does that mean?

She was allowed a visit in closed conditions. In open conditions the visits are held in the visitor room sitting across a table. In closed conditions it means the prisoner is cut off totally throughout the visit from the visitors and they have it in a closed visit area whereby they are kept totally separate but can speak to each other through a glass window.

The note records that Yvonne had quite a temper tantrum when initially refused?

Yes. When she was told she couldn't have a visit with this person, she started shouting, screaming, dashed off to her room and slammed the door.[113]

INMATE (19 YEARS OLD)

And did she throw her dinner at the walls in the sitting room?

Aye, she used to fling it at the walls. The staff weren't there at the time, so we just cleared up the mess and nobody says nothing about what happened.

How many times did this happen?

Twice.

Who cleaned up the mess?

Yvonne did. But the second time she got help from all of us, from all the lassies in the unit. And a member of staff asked who was responsible but we didn't tell it was Yvonne.[114]

GOVERNOR

What sort of signs would be signs of stress in a prisoner as far as you are concerned?

Perhaps not speaking or not eating. If they're normally withdrawn perhaps being extrovert. If they're normally extrovert, perhaps being withdrawn. Not speaking to people, not wanting to take visits, complaining when they're not normally the complaining type. A variety of different behaviours which as far as staff are concerned are not ordinary for that particular person.

What if a prisoner had been having temper tantrums and had been throwing her dinner at the wall, for example?

That would depend on the individual prisoner. For some, unfortunately, that's fairly standard behaviour.

If it was a prisoner who did not normally throw her dinner at the wall?

It would depend on what the circumstances were, if it was a row with another prisoner or if she had complained about the quality of her food and didn't get a satisfactory answer and decided to throw the food around, that's different from being under stress. One would need to know the prisoner in order to make a judgement.

One would also need to know why it was the prisoner had thrown her dinner at the wall?

Yes.[115]

PRISON PSYCHOLOGIST

How many times did you see Yvonne Gilmour altogether?

On one occasion only, the 12th of December.

Who initiated that meeting?

That came as a result of a medical officer referral to clinical psychology.

What was the purpose of the referral, do you know?

An assessment interview. I understood that Miss Gilmour's behaviour was somewhat aggressive on the block, and she was quite irritable.

Was it any part of your dealings at that meeting to assess her from the point of view of the prison's suicide prevention strategy?

Well, all staff are vigilant in that area, so any contact with an inmate would invariably involve the strategy coming into play. I did not see her specifically to assess her for suicide risk.

If we look at the entry you made in the mental health notes, is that in part a narrative of information that Yvonne Gilmour gave you in the course of the meeting?

Yes.

For example, it begins *Can't cope with normality. Always lose it.* Is that something she said?

It was in the conversation why she was using such an amount of drugs and her justification for this was that she couldn't cope with normality and that on embarking on a drug-free period she would then lose it.

When she was losing it, what was she losing, her temper, or her reason, or...?

Losing her ability to stay away from drugs.

A loss of self-control in that respect then?

No, not in that context, no.

But losing it meant what, that she was getting stoned or...?

Exactly, yes.

And then there follows a brief narrative of details about her background, her family, living in England...?

Yes, that's right.

And then there's a prison officer identified as giving good support. Do we take it she had nice things to say about this officer?

Oh, yes, particularly so.

Was she negative in any way about her relationship with staff?

No, she had singled out this officer, a female officer, and she said she got on better with the male staff. She obviously had certain complaints about the restrictions that the discipline staff have to impose but compared with other inmates' reports I wouldn't say Miss Gilmour's comments about staff were particularly pronounced. The only occasion she felt aggrieved I think was when she was reprimanded for shouting out a window at another inmate but she said she had been given just a verbal reprimand and she lost no privileges for that particular incident. She actually felt she was lucky to get away with just a verbal reprimand.

Then it says in the notes *At the end of the day, all our backgrounds are the same.* Do you remember the context of that remark?

Yes, I do. I spent about an hour with Miss Gilmour because

I felt initially she didn't seem pleased to see me, and her posture was quite hostile and she was avoiding eye contact, so a little bit longer was spent to establish some rapport with her. For that reason, I decided to just ask her about more general aspects, recent experiences and her experiences in prison before I looked at more focused aspects of her mental health. She was highlighting the similarity all the inmates seemingly have, the similar backgrounds, the similar level of drug use, the same fairly disordered backgrounds making a sort of philosophical statement about them all coming from the same reservoir, the same source.

And then there's a reference to sleeping okay and no problems with her appetite?

Yes, earlier she had said that her sleeping was disruptive and broken but later on she said it was okay. I described my professional role to her and told her I was not in a position to prescribe any further medication. I think then we moved on to a more true account of her mental state.

Did you get the impression that she thought she might be able to get a prescription from you?

Oh, yes.

Then there are references in the notes to previous suicide attempts – hanging, overdoses, slashes to wrists. Did she express any general attitude to these incidents?

She said that she had no real intent on these occasions and that she was glad to have been interrupted or disturbed or discovered. She tried to play down the incidents. She gave the impression that she was a bit embarrassed about them. She could readily recall them without feeling guilty.

Was she trying to play down the incidents, give you a false impression of their significance?

That's how she genuinely felt, that they were silly gestures. I can't say for what motivation, but she was certainly trying to divorce herself from them. I got the impression she regarded these incidents as a sign of immaturity.

And then there's a question that you posed her, are things getting better or worse for you?

She said she couldn't cope with reality and that's why she used illicit drugs outside of prison. She didn't have any job, no qualifications, her life was fairly chaotic and she felt that her friends were like her in the sense that they would abuse friendships to get more drugs and to use whatever they could to get more intoxicated.

Did she say anything about her ability to cope with life in prison?

Yes, she did. She said that she had a certain cultivated hard act within the prison. She had been in several prisons and wasn't prison naïve. I think she felt that she had created a tough façade that was helpful to her.

Did she give any indication that this was an act and that really she did find it difficult to cope?

No, because I think that I was struck by the fact that she was quite an assertive woman. She certainly was able to communicate very well with me and she was able to tell me interesting stories about previous experiences in prison which was just that she had never been particularly traumatised by prison experiences. She was actually quite blasé about the prospect of spending a further period of time in custody.

Then right at the foot of the first page of notes, there is something which I presume she told you. *I'm always told nothing is wrong with me.*

She said she had been in Leverndale and that the psychiatrist had said there was nothing wrong with her.

Did you ask her about suicide ideation?

Yes, I specifically did and I've noted that there was no suicidal behaviour or ideation.

You note that she said it was worse at night, trying to get to sleep?

I think this is a problem with people within the prison because prisons are extremely noisy and there can be times, specifically at night, when you are under-stimulated, when you are lacking the support of other inmates, and at night very often the reality of imprisonment tends to be most acute and problematic.

At the end, you have a section *Main problems at the moment: irritability, low mood, poor impulse control?*

I felt that these were three areas that I could potentially address or I could provide some input to. She acknowledged that she was irritable, that she was inclined to be a bit short with other inmates. She mentioned an incident with half a pint of milk where she had got quite short and bad-tempered with another inmate. She also said she was having difficulty controlling aggressive impulses. I also asked Miss Gilmour if she could possibly draw up a list of things she felt we could work on and she agreed to highlight some areas she was having difficulty with for a next visit.

Right at the end of the notes, it says *Do not think this girl will be likely to harm herself at present.* Did you actually discuss that with her?

Yes, she got asked that question that she had no current plans for engaging in suicidal behaviour and there was no ideation. Her entire presentation did not suggest to me that she was imminently in danger of engaging in a suicidal act. I would not predict whether somebody would be to a lesser or greater degree in danger of committing suicide. My assessment was confined to that day.

Did you discuss with her the prospects for ongoing treatment?

I said to her I would offer her a further session in which she would agree to engage in further treatment or not. Very often after the first meeting they will be able to make a decision whether or not they want to continue with clinical psychology intervention.

What was her attitude to that?

She indicated that she would certainly be happy to see me and she was aware that it would happen in the near future.

I had indicated to her it would be within two weeks. When I went back to my office, I consulted my diary and was able to put in a clinical slot for Miss Gilmour on the 19th of December.

Did you in fact see her on the 19th of December?

No, I did not. I had a clinic of six prisoners to see. When I arrived in the prison that morning, I saw three of the list and then I was told at twelve o'clock there had been security operations in the prison and I was confined to the health centre and was unable to see any further prisoners that day.

Did you make any further arrangement to see her after that?

No, I didn't. I consulted her notes and was aware that she was due in Court on the 23rd of December, therefore, she would automatically be seen by clinicians, including the medical officer.[116]

CHAPTER 17

December 1996 (contd.)

YVONNE

Form no. 259
Untried Prisoner's Letter

NOTICE CONCERNING COMMUNICATIONS WITH PRISONERS

All letters are read by the Authorities, who may keep them back if they think it is right to do so. Every letter will be kept back in the following cases:

If it is not written so as to be easily read
If it is not expressed in proper and temperate language
No unpaid letters will be received into the Prison.

H.M.Institution
Cornton Road
Stirling

Name: *Yvonne Gilmour*
Hall: *Yankee*

13.12.96

Dearest Linda,

Well, babes, I must say you looked really nice today and it was great seeing you, so thanks for coming up.

What happened to big Dave. I ain't even got any units left to ring you later but I'll try and get hold of some just for my girl.

Babes I promise you this: I'm gonna get my head together this time. I've got a woman that loves me and I'm in love with you, and there's no-one or anything going to take that away from me, or I will be doing time for killing some cunt and I promise I ain't gonna fuck you about because I'm in here. Most of the birds I wouldn't put the boot in but that's life, but apart from that you're my wife – and my life.

I'd die for you, you know I would.

I spoke to my lawyer today and fuck knows what's going on about this fine. He said they may just wait till the 23rd and see about it then. So still try and come up on Monday but ring first, alright. Bring a bit of hash just in case we get an open visit but I can't see it myself.

I miss you so much it hurts but this had to happen at some time. I just didn't think it would of happened like this. Still, they can't keep me here forever. Hey babes, so I'll be back in your loving arms before long.

This ain't gonna be a long letter as I've got loads to write i.e. my family!! I rang Carolann just after the visit and my little niece picked up the phone, which upset me a bit. God I love them kids so much and miss them like crazy. I just hope no-one comes to court apart from you.

I could go on all night writing but the tears are getting the better of me, so I'm gonna go for now and get this in the post. Hope to hear from you soon if not sooner.

Forever yours,
Gilly G.[117]

INMATE (16 YEARS OLD)

I was remanded to Cornton Vale on Friday 13th of December and Yvonne was already on remand in Y block where I was also put. I was just in the place and she skipped by my cell and came and introduced herself as Vonni G. She seemed to be very happy and cheery. I was very depressed at that time because I was only 16 and this was the first time I had ever been in jail and I knew I wasn't going to be with my family over Christmas. So I was really depressed. Yvonne got talking to me and asked me what I was in for, who I knew and things like that. She knew a friend of mine. She had met him in a rehab place in Helensburgh. We talked for a wee while in my room that first time and then when she was leaving, Yvonne turned back at the door and told me that by the way, she was a lesbian and had a girlfriend. She said she was just telling me because others would tell me anyway and she might as well hear it from me. I told Yvonne I didn't have a problem with that.

I got on really well with Yvonne. I would go to her cell and she would come into mine, playing music and things like that. I shared a cell with another girl but then I was put in the back cells with three other girls because I was so depressed. They put me in what the girls call triple sui-cells. These are cells for special suicide watches.

I still saw Yvonne when I was out and about and she seemed perfectly happy to me. She used to say to me that I was daft and that I wanted to get out one day. She used to get on at me for being on the triple suicide watch, saying I had a family to look after and that I should get my head down and get on with it. I remember one time I was on the phone to my mum and was getting a bit upset and Yvonne came and took the phone off me, spoke to my mum and told her I was OK in there and would be getting looked after.[118]

INMATE (30 YEARS OLD)

I knew Yvonne was having a relationship in prison with a girl called Cathy who was in the back cells in Unit 5 as a punishment for causing a disturbance in her own block. I don't know if Yvonne knew her before she came into the prison but I knew they were having a sort of relationship and Yvonne used to write a lot of letters to Cathy because she couldn't get to the part of the prison where Cathy was being held.

PRISON SUPERVISOR

Was there a problem about Yvonne Gilmour sharing during her period on remand in December?

There had been problems with who was sharing with Yvonne, yes.

What were these problems?

She could be quite a hard girl to get along with.

Are you saying it was hard to find people to share a cell with her?

It was hard to find people that were compatible.

Did Yvonne ever give you any indication of who she thought

was compatible with and who she would like to share a cell with?

Yes.

And what did she say in that regard?

Her friend Cathy Preston.

So Yvonne wanted to share with Cathy Preston.?

Yes.

And did she make that request to you?

Yes.

And you didn't agree to that request?

No.

Was there a reason why you didn't agree?

Cathy was being held in the back cells at that time.

Is that where people are held who have been a discipline problem?

Yes.

Is that the only reason you refused Yvonne's request to share?

Well, at that time, from what I recall, Cathy was a convicted prisoner. And there was no mixing between untried prisoners and convicted.

So a remand prisoner couldn't share a cell with a convicted prisoner?

Should not share, yes.

And once the remand prisoner had become a convicted prisoner would there be any reason why they could not have shared a cell?

Certainly not, if they were compatible, I wouldn't see it being a problem, no.

Would the fact that they were both lesbians bear any part in your assessment of their compatibility?

Yes, it probably would have, yes.

And how would that influence you?

It would be one factor in a lot of factors.

But would it be something that would make you automatically say no, that they couldn't?

No, it's not an automatic thing.

But it may be that in certain circumstances you might allow them to share?

Quite possibly, yes.[119]

INMATE (18 YEARS OLD)

You said she wasn't cheeky to the staff but she didn't like being told what to do?

She just didn't like being told what to do

What were the staff like to her in general?

Usually alright, some of them were alright.

And were some not alright?

Some of them are never alright.

But some of them were not alright with her?

Aye. You ken, it wasnae just Yvonne, it was everybody. It was just the way they were with everybody.

Did it have anything to do with the fact that Yvonne was a lesbian, the way the staff treated her?

No, not at all.[120]

INMATE (30 YEARS OLD)

Now you've told us you were visiting in another cell when Yvonne Gilmour came in?

It was a weekend. I think it was a Sunday night.

Did you speak to her when she came into the cell?

Yes, just 'How's things?' and that, what you usually say to the girls when you walk into a cell. You don't really know them and that, I mean, so it was just 'How's things?' and that.

What sort of mood was Yvonne Gilmour in?

Laughing.

Did she do anything when she came into the cell?

She was just talking to the girls there and she stood on the chair at the window to see if, she was just like that, laughing, and 'Do you think I could hang myself frae here?' It was like a carry on.

She was joking about hanging herself?

Uh huh.

How did that come about? Had there been any ...?

Naebody says nothing in the room. She just stood on the chair, bounced on it, laughing.

Did she say anything while she was doing this?

Just laughing. She was jumping to see if she could reach the bars. She was quite a big girl anyway. She said something like 'Well, do you think I could hang myself from here?' And one of the lassies said 'That's no' funny'.

What did Yvonne Gilmour do then?

She jumped down from the chair then she stayed about five minutes, then she left. We a' took it as a joke, the way she was doing it. It was just like a joke and she was carrying on. We never took it serious.

How would you describe her generally during this remand period?

She was brand new.

Did she ever complain about anything to you?

No' really, no.

Was there something then?

It was just that her girlfriend Cathy was down the back stairs and she was running back and forward to her quite a lot, and she wasn't allowed to, but she was going out of her way to try her best to get down there and she cried about it, but she went to her own room and cried, and that was the end of it. You know what I mean? She never really spoke about it because I went to her room and I asked her if she wanted to speak about it and she says no. There was nothing we could do or say if she didn't want to speak.

Yes?

And there was another time that she tried to get away to see Cathy. That was when Cathy was out for a bath. I think they get out for an hour. You get sent for a bath, tea and whatever you need, a change of clothes and that. And Yvonne sneaked in to see her and was caught actually in the bathroom with her. And an officer told her to go back to her unit and she was placed on report, which would happen to any of the rest of us.

Was Yvonne then confined to her cell?

Aye, she was locked in because she was told to stay back from Cathy and she went out of her way to go down to the other unit although she was told no' to go, she had to stay in her own unit. I asked her if she was okay. I looked through the spyhole and she had her head in her hands and she said 'Just leave me alone'.

Was there another occasion when Yvonne got upset about Cathy?

Yvonne had given Cathy a lend of her phone card and Cathy used the whole card which Yvonne didnae find funny. And Cathy got a pair of trainers from her other girlfriend and Yvonne was upset and wrote Cathy a letter and gave it to one of the wee lassies to take it down the back stairs and then she walked away crying.[121]

MICHELLE

Yvonne phoned me on the 16th of December. It was a Monday. She asked me to send her two Christmas cards with 'girlfriend' on them and a packet of cards for other people. I asked her how many girlfriends she had and she said, 'You know me. You know what it's like, one in here and one out there.' She also asked if I could send money to her because being on remand she wasn't working and I said that if I had it I would. After that she told me she loved me and I told her the same. She told me she would phone again. She was a bit upset because she was in jail for Christmas and she missed us. I told her to cheer up and look after herself.

YVONNE

Form no. 259
Untried Prisoner's Letter

NOTICE CONCERNING COMMUNICATIONS WITH PRISONERS

All letters are read by the Authorities, who may keep them back if they think it is right to do so. Every letter will be kept back in the following cases:

If it is not written so as to be easily read
If it is not expressed in proper and temperate language
No unpaid letters will be received into the Prison.

H.M.Institution
Cornton Road
Stirling

Name: *Yvonne Gilmour*
Hall: *Yankee* 18.12.96

Darling Linda,

Yvonne on the bill and ben with the news at ten!

Well, I rang you four times today and told them I'd ring back but every time I rang back, you didn't come down. My head's that up my I can't even remember if I did talk to you?

I rang my sister tonight. Carolann and the kids came on the phone and that really did my head in.

There's a lot of things on my mind at the moment but please don't think I don't want you cos I do and I love you so much it's hurting inside and I cry myself to sleep at night wishing I was next to my No.1 girl. So please, please don't worry cos my love for you will never die. I need you just as much as you need me, but I promise I ain't taking the piss. You mean too much for me to do that. I swear I'm gonna stay drug free and when I get out it's me and you (When I get out?). I'm just keeping my head down thinking of you 24.7 and that is it... Keep in touch with my sister Michelle and you know you're more than welcome up at her house even for Christmas if you want.

Well, I'm gonna get my head down cos I need to dream a dream of me and you, but I'll be up first thing in the morning on the bill and ben. I've got some sounds for the night and I hope I hear our song as I still haven't heard it.

Step by step, day by day, I'm still with my girl all the way.
Missing you
Gilly G[122]

MICHELLE

On the Friday she phoned about teatime. She said she was at court on the Monday and that she didn't want anyone to go and see her. I don't think she wanted us to know why she was in prison and she didn't want us to see her getting upset. I told her that she was alright and she would be okay. She said she didn't want us to go up in case it upset her to see us. She wasn't on for long.

CAROLANN

On the Friday before Christmas, before it happened, Yvonne called me in the morning. She was a bit upset and said she was going to court on the Monday. She told me not to go to court and was quite specific about that. She began to cry and said she wouldn't be out for a while. She said she wouldn't be out for my birthday and my daughter's birthday in March. I told her she was not to worry and that that was a long way away. She never mentioned the prison again but was more concerned about what would happen at the court. She told me she would book the phone to call me back at seven o'clock that night to talk again. I think Yvonne thought she was going to get a long sentence and was unhappy about that. I think she had got herself worked up about that.

Yvonne didn't phone me back that night so I thought that she may have phoned someone else. That's why it didn't worry me that she hadn't phoned back.

YVONNE

19.12.96

Well my girl,

It's me again with a few lines so I can get this posted today. Sorry I haven't wrote much but I haven't really wrote to anyone. I just can't get my head round it. I took three fits yesterday and two the day before. I feel fuck all the time. Rita said she was going to write to me cos I've only had letters off my girl but I don't care if no-one else writes as long as you do.

Paula said she was going to come to court but we'll see. As long as I see you I don't give two fucks about anyone else.

I told my family not to come but they don't know what court I'm at anyway so that's alright, hey.

Linda, please don't worry about a thing cos its always gonna be you and me alright? Well I'm gonna love you and leave you cos my hand is hurting me just like my heart.

I love you darling
Gilly G.

Bye bye babes.
See you Monday.[123]

INMATE (29 YEARS OLD)

Not getting to see her girlfriend, that really did her nut in. I remember once I was sitting in my room along with another girl when Yvonne came in. She'd been caught trying to get to see Cathy and I remember her saying 'I'll give then the shock of their fucking lives when they open that door in the morning.' I told her to shut up and not be so stupid talking like that.

And she said she was only kidding and then she just went on being her normal self.[124]

INMATE (29 YEARS OLD)

Yvonne had been locked in her room for throwing her dinner against the wall and the next day I was talking to her along with another girl and Yvonne said something like 'I'll give them the shock of their lives, I'm going to swing from the bars.' She said it in a kind of joking manner. I remember the other girl said 'Aye, so you will.' Neither of us took it seriously.

YVONNE

Cathy,

That's me behind my wood for the night cos I put my dinner all over the walls. Cunts, they're just playing mind games with me and you, fucking cunts. I'm trying my hardest to keep ma head about it but I can't cope really, no matter how hard I try, I'm letting them get to me in a big way. I wish I had you here with me cos I'm missing you like crazy and believe me it's in more ways than one. I'm hurting so much it's killing me inside and out. I swear I keep looking at the bars, but believe me it's only you that's stopping me from doing it. You're all I've got, Cathy, I better stop talking like that cos I will end up doing it, knowing me and it wouldn't be a cry for help cos I'd be a goner, fucking hell, I'm letting them get to me, hey babes. Don't worry, Cathy, I will not do anything silly, I promise you, I love you too much for a start. You know, they keep looking in on me every few minutes cos one of the girls said she's gonna hang herself (fucking cunts).

Hi, I'm back. They let me out to use the telephone to ring my dad and sisters so it's about 9.30p.m. and I'm missing you more every minute of the day. I feel so helpless cause I'm just around the corner but if there's anything you need just let me know and I'll do my best for my number one girl. I swear I'm sick of lock up.

Cathy loves Nora on my bed? I hope on your bed it's my name and not hers. Still, I don't care cos I've got you now and let anyone try and take you away from me, I swear I'll kill them!

Well, my girl, I'm going to try and get my head down. I need to know if you'll be going back to your unit before I go to Court. So try and find out.

I'll be back on the bill and ben with the news at ten in the morning.

Sweet dreams, love you,
YG
7.45a.m.
Good Morning!

So about this letter. My head was up my arse all day yesterday and them cunts didn't help matters much, so do forgive me. I love you and can't wait to see you tomorrow. Well, that's us getting out so I'll write more tomorrow.

Don't forget,
Love ya,
Your No.1 girl,
YG[125]

PRISON SUPERVISOR

Yvonne had a friend who was located in the segregation cells in the same block as Yvonne, a very close friend. Yvonne told me that she and Cathy, her friend, were lesbian. Cathy was on a Rule 80,which means she was taken out of association for subversive activities on the convicted side. Cathy was a convicted prisoner and convicted and untried are not allowed to mix, but Cathy was in the same block as Yvonne, although in a different unit at the other end, but Yvonne had approached me on a number of occasions over the weekend asking if she could go and see Cathy. Initially, it was just a flat no. 'No, she is convicted, Yvonne, you cannot see her. You know that convicted and non-tried don't get mixing.' But Yvonne knew me and I knew Yvonne and she was like 'Please, Miss, come on, let me go down.' So, eventually over the course of the weekend, Yvonne was going to Court on the Monday morning and I was on duty all weekend and I said to her 'On the Sunday prior to you being locked in for the night, I'll let you go down and you can speak to her, but I will not open the segregation door. I'll allow you to speak to her through the door. You will not see her face to face.' I was bending the rules slightly but it wasn't going to do any harm.

Yvonne was delighted with this, went away, came back on the Sunday night, 'Can I go now, can I go now, can I go now?' and I says 'No, a wee bit later, a wee bit later' and eventually 'yes'. We went down, I let her speak to Cathy through the door, and that was fine. It was just about her going to Court and telling Cathy to look after herself and not to worry about Yvonne. She had to shout all this through the door. When she was finished, she came back up, thanked me very much, said she felt much better, and that was it.

I was on early shift the next morning and Yvonne was among the girls getting ready to go to Court. So she came along, could she go back down, could she go back down. I said 'No, you got last night and that's it' and we had a laugh between ourselves about it. 'Oh, come on, you know I only want to say cheerio' and I said 'You are taking liberties' and she was laughing 'No, no, I'm not' and she waited until I wasn't looking and she ran down the back to the segregation unit and I heard the voices, then she came running up and I said to her 'Oh, who is taking liberties now?' 'Sorry, ' she said, hands up, 'I'll go to Court.' She had scored a point, she thought, and I mean, to be honest, it hadn't cost me anything. She thought she had got something. We had a laugh about her taking liberties, and that was it. The last thing she asked me before she left for Court was to remember to keep an eye on Cathy. 'I'm worried about her,' she said. She was really concerned about her, how she would deal with lack of association. She said, 'Look keep an eye on Cathy, Miss, I'm worried about her.'[126]

INMATE (23 YEARS OLD)

Was Yvonne Gilmour your girlfriend?

Yes.

During the period that Yvonne was in prison did she ever say to you that she was upset because prison officers had been unpleasant about the fact that she was gay?

No, she never actually said that to me but she would just get like wee smart remarks, like myself. She says, *The staff were giving me pelters because I tried to get down to see you, Cathy, because we are going with each other.*

Can you explain to us what the word 'pelters' means?

Just saying 'What are you doing going with her?' I mean just stupid things like that, you know, what are you two doing going with each other, it was just things like that.

And when Yvonne told you about these pelters, was it something she was upset about?

No. The two of us just used to take that in our stride, you know what I mean, laugh that off, that's nothing.

When Yvonne Gilmour was admitted into Cornton Vale on the 9th of December, she was remanded into Yankee Block? Which block were you in?

Bravo Block.

Did you see Yvonne at that time?

I never actually seen her. It was just looking out of the window and shouting to each other in passing. I never got the chance to speak to her.

Now you got moved from Bravo Block to Yankee Block. Was there a specific reason for the move?

Yes, I was in a bit of trouble in Bravo and so I got moved to Yankee.

You were put in some sort of discipline cell in Yankee?

Yes.

Did you see Yvonne after you had been moved?

Yes. When I was getting out for like baths and getting my washing done and things.

How many times did you see her?

I can only say roughly, a few times anyway.

Did you get the chance to speak to her?

I never really got to speak to her much because the officer that was there, she used to always grab me going back, 'You were speaking to Yvonne, you can't speak to Yvonne', but I always used to shout from a distance.

How did Yvonne seem? How was her mood?

Every time I seen Yvonne, she was carrying on, laughing, carrying on with me to keep me happy, you know, when I was ever out of my cell to go for a bath or that, Yvonne would cheer me up.

Yes?

Because like when you are down the back cells you are by yourself all the time, you are never with anybody.

Right?

And she was just trying to keep me happy, cheer me up. That's why she sent so many letters, you know, so that I would have something to read and that.

Were you supposed to be in segregation, with no contact with other inmates?

Yes. But Yvonne used to write me letters. And I was writing to Yvonne *When you get out, we'll try and make a go of it. And I'll help you to get away from drugs.* She was invited to stay with me and my family so she could get the chance to stay away from drugs.

Did you see Yvonne on the day she went to Court, on the 23rd of December?

I was still locked up at the time she went to Court but she came, one of the officers let her come down to the door and speak to me before she went to Court. It was about quarter to seven in the morning.

And what did she speak about?

She just says she was going to Court and she was expecting a sentence, she would see me when she came back because I thought that I would have been off the rule I was on and back in Bravo Block, which I wasn't when she came back. She must have knew she was getting a sentence, she just said, 'I'll see you when I get back tomorrow night' I said, 'I hope no'. I hope you get out, Yvonne.' And she was like that, 'No, no. Hopefully I'll see you in Bravo tonight' because I was on punishments for 72 hours, which would have took me to Monday, and it was reviewed. And then I was to stay on punishments till my lib date.

What sort of mood was Yvonne in that morning?

She was in a happy mood because she was like, I will see you when I come back and we will be able to get a better talk when I get back.

Did you see her again at all after that occasion?

I seen her on Christmas Eve, in the afternoon. I was getting taken to the health centre and she was getting brought up to the health centre at the same time so I was sitting speaking to her. I was actually upset that day. Yvonne was comforting me, she got out a travel agent's calendar, everything was going to be alright because I had been took away from the rest of the prison and I was a bit upset about it. Yvonne was comforting me, asking me if I was alright, and she gave me a cuddle. She was trying to cheer me up. She was laughing, she was saying to me, cheer up, you are strong, just try and get on with it. She said she would try and see me before I get out, and that was it.

How were things left between you at the end of the meeting in the health centre?

Everything was fine because I asked Yvonne to get a visitor's pass for me because I was due out on Friday and I said to Yvonne to get a visit pass for Sunday and I'll come up and see you and she was like, that's brilliant but I'll phone you before Sunday.

So you were suggesting that you would come and visit her in Cornton Vale the weekend after Christmas because you were getting out on the Friday?

That's right.

Now you mentioned that you got a number of letters from Yvonne?

Yes.

Now I want you to look at one letter. In this letter she writes

***I am trying my hardest to keep my head about but I can't cope, really no matter how hard I try I am letting them get to me in a big way.* Do you recognise this letter as a letter you got from Yvonne Gilmour?**

Yes.

Do you remember when you got the letter?

I can't remember the date exactly. I remember getting it and one of the officers on the block, well, the rest of the girls on the block had been away somewhere at a disco or something so they let me out for a bath when they were away and this officer he mentioned something to me 'Your pal round the corner is trying to get round to see you'. I said 'What pal?' and he went, 'She was trying to get round to see you, she's round there acting like a big baby because she can't get round to see you.'

She writes in the letter *They're just playing mind games with me and you.* Can you help us with what she meant by that?

Because they knew Yvonne was desperate to get to see me, even just to talk to me with the door open, see me face to face, even by my door, but they were like that, *No, you're no' going down, you're no' going down* kind of things like that. I mean, they knew how much it was hurting her and they just werenae letting her even for a couple of minutes they werenae letting her, that kind of thing. And it's they way they talk to you, just being cheeky, snide remarks, just talking to you as if they're better, that kind of thing. For instance, there was one day I was out for a bath and Yvonne's like that *Can I just see her for two minutes?* And Miss Ross that was on duty she goes *You are seeing nobody for two minutes, just get in your bloody cell and you'll see her whenever.* They would just speak to you like that.

How did you actually get the letter?

Somebody actually put it under the door of my cell for me. One of the lassies. I recognised her voice. She said through the spyhole, 'You've got a letter from Yvonne'.

The letter goes on, *I'm hurting so much, it is killing me inside and out and I swear I keep looking at the bars but believe me it's only you that's stopping me from doing it.* Were you worried about Yvonne Gilmour when you read that?

I didn't take any notice of it because she didn't come across as that sort of person because I have heard loads of people in the prison say that, I have said it myself, just the way I was feeling that day, but you have to put up with it.

And if we read the bit at the end, where she says *My head was up my arse,* it sounds as if maybe Yvonne Gilmour's mood changed in the morning after she'd written the letter?

Yes.

Did you tell anyone about letter after you got it, or mention it to the staff?

No.

I would like you to look at another letter from Yvonne to you? Have you got that?

Yes.

And it starts *Just to let you know I am out on the 21st January but there is still the fine of £250.* Is that right?

Yes.

So it looks as if this letter is telling you what happened at Court?

Well, yes.

Do you know when you got this letter?

I can't remember. I'm not sure.

Well, do you know which of the letters you got first, the one you have in front of you at the moment or the other one we were looking at a moment ago?

The other one. I can't remember getting this letter at all.

Which letter?

This one. This is the first time I've seen it.

Are you sure about that?

Yes, I didn't even know Yvonne's lib date. That's how I know I didn't get that letter. This is the first time I've seen it.

Yvonne Gilmour

Same address
Different day

Hi sexy,

Just to let you know I'm out on the 21st Jan but there's still the fine for £250 but I'm going to try and get up to court before I get out, or they will be waiting at the gate for me.

Well, it was great seeing you today but it also hurt me to see you that way but you can do it, please babes do it for us.

I love you, never forget that. You will not get in to see me on Sunday cos you know the score. But we will see. Babes, don't worry about tomorrow cos I swear I'm staying in my room all day thinking of you only because my love for you is true.

Love ya and miss ya more than words can say
YG

P.S. I need your address for when you get out.[127]

MICHELLE

About 6 o'clock on Monday the 23rd, Yvonne phoned me again. This time she was really upset and crying. She told me she had got 3 months and would be out in January, the 14th. I told her, 'Well, a couple of weeks time and that's you done'. Before she knew it she would be home. 'Don't worry about it' is all I says to her. I told her she could come back to me and Yvonne said she wanted to come back. But it was Christmas and she kept saying she didn't want to be in jail for Christmas. She wanted to be with her family. I told her we'd have her Christmas when she got out. But she kept saying she didn't want to be in for Christmas and I kept saying it would be alright, she would be okay, January was just round the corner. But she was really upset about being in for Christmas. She was upset but never said she would do harm to herself. I told her that when she got out we would paint the town red, or at least my house. She laughed at this. I told her not to do anything silly and she said she wouldn't. She said, 'I'll send visitor passes out for you and dad and that and will you bring the kids up' meaning her nieces and her nephew. The last thing I said to her was 'Yvonne, don't do anything stupid' meaning don't get in any more trouble or get extra time for bad behaviour or anything so that she could come out on the 14th or whatever day her release date was. She said, 'I won't, I promise' and the last thing she says to me was she loved me. Then she was away because I think she said there was a queue for calls. That was the last I heard from her.

CAROLANN

On Monday 23rd December, about tea-time that night, Yvonne phoned me again and told me she had got three months. I replied 'Good' but didn't mean it in a bad way. I meant that at least it wasn't six months or something. I think that she maybe took it the wrong way because she said that the sentence was bad enough. I explained to her what I meant and she seemed to accept that. She told me she would be out in January and I said 'Well, there you go. January is just round the corner.' Yvonne sounded a wee bit down but wasn't crying or anything. I asked her if she had got the Christmas cards that my dad and I had sent and she said she hadn't. She did say that this was maybe because she had been at court.

PART FIVE

Christmas in Prison

CHAPTER 18

23rd December

INMATE (16 YEARS OLD)

I was in the Triple S cells for most of my remand time. I tried to kill myself on the 23rd I think it was. I was out mixing with the others and had just gone through a wee door at the back cells. This is a wee half narrow door and once through that you go upstairs to where they change all the bulbs. I tried to hang myself from the rafters there, using my dressing gown. We got the dressing gown, we just didn't get the belt to tie it. I don't remember getting found, someone told me it had broken and I fell. I think it was Yvonne's girlfriend Cathy Preston who told the screws she had heard me go through the wee door. I was told by the prison afterwards to keep it quiet as the door should have been locked but as far as I know it was open all the time. This door was beside the triple suicide cells and the screws said the jail had a bad enough reputation, never mind for getting a name for negligence, leaving doors open at the suicide cell.

I was eventually liberated at the beginning of January. My case was adjourned but I'll probably be remanded again because I missed my psychiatric appointment because I had to go to a funeral. I am better prepared for jail this time. It was a shock and a bit scary the first time because I was so young and because it was Christmas but I think I'll be able to deal with it better this time.[128]

INMATE (24 YEARS OLD)

On the way back from Court on the 23rd, I was handcuffed to Yvonne because she had asked the police if she could get on the cuff with me. There was another girl handcuffed to us as well but I can't remember her name. Yvonne was in the middle. Yvonne was as happy as Larry because she got a three month sentence and she had been expecting at least six. When we got to the prison reception, we were all put into individual dog boxes to be stripped and searched. Yvonne was told that she was going to be put in Sierra for induction and she wasn't pleased. I heard her crying, shouting and screaming from her box and answering the screws back when they spoke to her. She was swearing and shouting 'Fuck, cunt, bastards' that sort of language. I was two boxes away from her and I shouted to her and asked her if she was alright. She shouted 'Aye' but she was still crying. She wanted to be in the same block as her girlfriend. Yvonne went on like this for about five minutes or a bit longer and another girl who was with us said to the screws that they should do something to calm Yvonne down but they left her to get on with it. Maybe because she had been cheeky to them.

PRISON OFFICER

On the 23rd of December in the evening you were on duty in the reception area carrying out admission interview procedure. Did you have dealings with a newly arriving inmate called Yvonne Gilmour?

Yes. She was returning, she had went out to Court that morning and had came back convicted.

Do you have a term to describe somebody in that position?

A technical admission.

Where did Yvonne Gilmour go when she first arrived in the reception area?

She was placed in the box, she would have the same box that she went out from in the morning. She was placed in the box and she would be told to get stripped, technicals don't have showers, and we would strip search her and she would get dressed again and go and see the nurse.

When the prisoner has stripped, do you then go into the holding cell and check that they don't have any weapons or drugs or anything of that nature?

Yes, they strip, they stand with their backs to us and we go in with a dressing gown. They put the dressing gown on, we check their feet and their mouths, their body and their clothing. Then they get dressed again.

Did you have any trouble with Yvonne that night?

She was fine to start with. Myself and the other officer on duty were dealing with what blocks the girls were going to and Yvonne was wandering about the reception area and overheard us, overheard me saying that Yvonne would go to induction, where all the admissions go, and Yvonne started getting irate and said she wanted to go to Bravo, and I sat and explained to her that all admissions had to go to induction, which is Sierra, but she would maybe get put to Bravo the next day, it would be up to the induction staff, but she wasnae happy that she was having to go to induction.

You said that she was walking about the reception area? Are the girls at liberty to walk around?

Yes, well, if the girls are quiet and are no' causing any problems, their doors get left open and they can sit and they can go an' get their cups of tea and stuff to eat. If they are no' causing a problem, then yes, their doors are left open and they can sit in the same box and blether if they want. Since December we've done away with those boxes, now it's just one big holding room.

Can you describe Yvonne's behaviour when she found out she was going to Sierra?

At first, she was just saying she wanted to go to Bravo and I explained to her that all admissions had to go to induction in Sierra and she just wasn't having this and she was getting more and more irate. Eventually I put her in her box because we had to get on with our work. I tried to speak to her, I tried to tell her what's the problem, you ken, you're only going for one night. But she didn't want to speak to me. I was the bad one because I wasnae letting her go to Bravo, where she wanted to be.

Was she upset in terms of crying?

Yes, she was crying when I was putting her in her box and

shouting. That behaviour was unusual for my dealings with Yvonne, she was never like that before.

Did she quieten down after that?

She went on shouting for about five minutes then the nurse came for her next person and she took Yvonne because she could see Yvonne was as high as a kite.

How long did she spend with the nurse?

She was in quite a while but I don't know exactly how long.

And what happened when she came back out of the nurse's room?

I would say she was even worse. She was crying and shouting that she definitely wanted to go to Bravo and the nurse locked her back in her holding box. She was there until the officer came to take her to Sierra.[129]

PRISON NURSE

I saw Yvonne Gilmour on Monday 23rd December. She came in with about eight others that evening. She was a technical admission, having gone out of the prison for a Court appearance that morning. We tend to do the technical admissions first because there isn't as much paperwork. She was in a cubicle in the reception area. I took her from there to the nurses' interview room. She was very upset and crying. When I asked her what was upsetting her, she said she was very angry because she was going to be sent to Sierra Block that evening. She said that she had been abused as a child and that in Sierra Block she was aware there was a woman whose offences were of a sexual nature against children. I told her I would speak to the reception staff and ask them what was happening to Yvonne that night. I left her in the interview room briefly and spoke to the officers on duty at reception. They confirmed that Yvonne was to go to Sierra and that they were aware that Yvonne was upset. I tried to reassure Yvonne that the staff would be made aware of the situation, that they would try and keep them apart and I thought they would not keep her in Sierra longer than they had to, and that seemed to pacify her a little. I completed a Prevention of Suicide (POS) form for Yvonne. She said, as I have noted on the form, that she had attempted to hang herself six years before. I asked her if she really wanted to die, if this was a serious suicide attempt. Yvonne said that at that time she probably did but was glad the attempt had not been successful as she had made numerous attempts and she felt that these were just attention-seeking behaviour to draw attention to her unhappy circumstances at the time. She said that she was very unhappy when she was young and she tried to kill herself many times but these were mostly attention-seeking.

I checked the background indicators on the form for history of psychiatric treatment, drug misuse, alcohol misuse, little contact with her family as positive. Five of the seven past risk indicators were checked as positive, but just because there's a lot of risk factors highlighted in the form, I think it's important to assess the person as you find them on the night.

Under the present risk indicators, the only positive one was *Talks of Suicide*. When I questioned her, she denied any suicidal intentions. I further questioned her in order to reassure myself that she was no cause for concern and discussed the recent instances at Cornton Vale. Yvonne told me she could understand why girls did these things, because of the pressures they were under, but she totally denied any idea of self harm and said she had too much to live for. She did not threaten suicide, and we talked of suicide and she talked quite openly about suicidal matters. She said she was glad she was in prison, that she would get help coming off drugs and I said it wasn't easy and she agreed and said she could understand why girls hung themselves because they were in jail withdrawing from drugs. I asked her if she'd ever felt like harming herself when she was in the jail because she was coming off drugs and she said yes, she had thought about it but that wasn't anything that she would consider now. I was not concerned about her being a risk of suicide that night, but I did feel that she talked about it a lot, and that's why I selected that option. She was much calmer at the end and I took her back to the main reception area and left her there getting a cup of tea.

After that I phoned the block to say that Yvonne was upset because she was being sent to Sierra Block, that she was worried about doing some harm to a prisoner who was already there because of the crime she had committed but despite the fact she was upset, I did not think she was suicidal and she was only on general observation.

Could you look at the POS form filled in for Yvonne's admission by another nurse in July of that year? You will see that the nurse at admission then, some six months previously, has put in under *Previous Suicides* 'Two years, attempted hanging'?

Yes.

So there is quite a big difference in timing, between the two years, mentioned there and the six years on the form you completed?

Yes.

Now the other nurse has told us that that information came from Yvonne herself, and we've heard from you that the six years came from Yvonne?

Yes.

Now if you take it from me that the two years is the more accurate of the timings, what does that tell you about the information that Yvonne gave to you?

It wasn't reliable.

And had you known that at the time of your interview with her, would you have followed it up?

Yes. I would have questioned her further. I would have said that I had this information and she was telling me different information now, why was this.

If you had had this form from the July admission, and if it was in the medical records at the time when you prepared your interview with Yvonne, you would have had that information that there was a discrepancy in time?

Yes.

So would you agree that it would be useful to have on your pris-

oner's medical file previous POS forms even if they do not result in placing someone on suicide strategy?

Yes.

Had you had that information, you said you would have asked her more questions. You can't say where that would have taken you, what the outcome would have been but it may have been that her answers would have been such that you would have been concerned about her and you may have put her in the at risk category?

I may have done, yes.

I mean you would have placed her on the suicide prevention strategy?

Yes. That may have been the outcome, yes.[130]

English Prison Records

15/7/94

At approx 20.20 hrs on 15/7/94 during bell-testing I found Yvonne Gilmour with a ligature round her neck. She was semi-conscious. A genuine attempt at suicide by hanging.

20/7/94

Found to be suspended by neck from ligature from window bars. Taken to hospital wing. There was a note. This was a serious attempt.[131]

PRISON OFFICER

It wasn't the first time I had met Yvonne Gilmour. The first time, in fact, was on the day that the last suicide happened, at the beginning of September. Yvonne was admitted to prison the same day it happened.

I was on duty in induction in Sierra on the 23rd of December when Yvonne was brought over from reception. I had received a phone call from the nurse in reception that Yvonne was in a bad mood and not happy about coming to Sierra. When I went through the administration paperwork with

Yvonne, she was quite aggressive. Her answers were short and curt. I asked Yvonne the reason why she did not want to be in Sierra and she replied 'I don't want to be in a unit where there is a fucking beast'. She said she didn't want to talk about it and I wasn't to take it personally. I said she needed to talk about it to the doctor or nurse in the morning and she said she would think about it. I told her she would not be put in the same unit as the prisoner and she would in fact be on a different floor. I said I would leave a note for the early shift to try and have Yvonne moved to Bravo the next day. Yvonne then apologised for her behaviour and appeared to accept the arrangements. It didn't take her long to calm down and then she seemed normal, which is how I knew her from her incarceration in September.[132]

INMATE (48 YEARS OLD)

I met Yvonne in Sierra the day she came in. She came onto the communal sitting room and asked for a light for her cigarette. She just asked everyone in general. I said, 'I've got a light here, hen' and she took a light from me. Then she turned to this other prisoner, Helen Carr, and started going on about the offence she had committed, calling her names, that sort of thing. She called her a beast, which is what they call a child molester, and she was also calling her other names. Yvonne seemed extremely upset. Helen Carr was known for her offences against children and got a lot of abuse from other inmates as well and in fact before I got released someone burned her.

Despite being called names by Yvonne, Helen Carr never gave any reaction. It didn't last all that long the whole situation. When she was finished with the verbal abuse, Yvonne just left the room.[133]

INMATE (23 YEARS OLD)

I first met Yvonne in August in Cornton Vale. We just used to say hello to each other in passing but as time went on Yvonne used to come down from her unit to my unit and we used to sit and chat, a crowd of us together until such times as we got caught, as it was against the rules for prisoners to move from one unit to another. I thought Yvonne was a very nice girl although she and I did not really talk much and we never discussed her private life or mine either for that matter.

She didn't seem to be out of prison all that long before she was back in again. I saw her at the health centre about the second week in December. She said she was on remand. She was very full of herself that day and was just going back and forth continually looking out of the window. She just would not stay at peace or even in one place and she seemed very impatient as if she was desperate to return to her unit. She was constantly being told by the officers to sit down but she kept getting back up again. She was cheery enough.

The next time I saw her was in Sierra Block on 23rd December. Yvonne was actually upstairs and I was downstairs. On that evening I was in the television room with quite a few other girls and Yvonne came in and just stood there in the middle of the room and then she suddenly turned round and looked over towards me and called me a beast and said that she was going to kill me and that I'd better get out of the unit before she did. The threat didn't bother me because I've had quite a few of those threats from other prisoners in Cornton Vale, obviously because of my convictions for lewd and libidinous practices. I took it that Yvonne had found out why I was in prison. After that, she just turned and walked out of the room. I didn't report the matter.

PRISON OFFICER

When I arrived in Unit 3 Sierra Block I saw a female I didn't know and who I took to be Yvonne Gilmour standing talking to another prisoner outside the office. This sort of behaviour has always been discouraged and so I asked the two girls if I could be of assistance. The other girl turned and immediately walked away but Yvonne Gilmour retorted looking me up and down, 'I don't think so'. This was said in an aggressive and facetious manner. She then went to the sitting room a few steps along the corridor and I followed her. I had been told by reception staff that she had made an open threat against another inmate and I was wary of her causing a disturbance. When I entered the sitting room, Yvonne turned and walked out. I had seen no exchange between her and Helen Carr, the prisoner she had threatened to harm, who was also in the sitting room. I did note, however, that Helen Carr was as white as a sheet about her face and she was shaking. I asked her if she was alright and she said 'This will be the worst Christmas of my life.'

CHAPTER 19

Christmas Eve

FORMER PRISON MEDICAL OFFICER

Have you in the past served as a Medical Officer at Cornton Vale Prison?

Yes, I worked part-time there, one half day a week, from 1989 until December 1996.

On the morning of the 24th of December last year do you remember seeing Yvonne Gilmour at the prison health centre in connection with what was called a technical admission?

I do, yes.

What sort of mood was Yvonne in when you met her?

Angry.

How did the anger manifest itself?

Her first thing was a verbal attack on the nurse saying *Are you the nurse that admitted me last night?* Very aggressively. To which the nurse replied *I never saw you until I gave you your medication last night.* I thought when she came in she was going to attack the nurse.

What happened next?

I then asked Yvonne why she was angry, was it about her sentence and she said no, she'd got a three-month sentence and she'd been expecting a six-month sentence. And I went on to try and find out why she was so upset and she was upset about which block she'd been put in and who else was in the block with her.

You have recorded something in your note of the meeting about that. I think what's recorded here is *I was sexually abused as a child, I'm going to fucking murder the beast they've locked me up with.*

Yes.

Is that what Yvonne said, verbatim?
Those were her words to me.
Was she speaking in a raised voice?
A firm voice.
Did she swear?
She told me she was going to fucking murder the beast, if that counts as swearing.
Did she remain in the same mood throughout the meeting?
She calmed down a bit once I had ascertained whether the disciplinary staff knew that she was upset and she said they did. I asked if there was anything else that was upsetting her, did she want to see the psychologist she'd seen before and she said yes she wanted treatment from him. I asked her whether it being Christmas Eve made me think it unlikely that she'd get it until the New Year and she said yes, that would be okay in the New Year, she just wanted to continue. I recorded her request in the medical notes.
Did she discuss with you why she wanted to see the psychologist?
No, that's confidential between her and the psychologist, a lot of it. I was just checking that she wanted all her psychological treatment. The psychologist had written in the notes that he would be happy to see her for treatment.
You have initialled and dated Yvonne Gilmour's POS form. Did you have a chance to look at it before you saw her?
Yes.
The nurse has recorded there *Attempted hanging, six years ago, Barnwood Hall.* You will have seen that at the time of your interview with her?
Yes, that was six years ago when she was sixteen. She was subsequently seen by psychiatrists who didn't feel that she had mental illness or was going to hurt herself in the more recent past.
Did you actually speak to Yvonne about this matter?
No, I didn't discuss it with her.

The nurse also recorded Yvonne's stay in Leverndale for psychiatric assessment. Did you discuss that with Yvonne?

No. But I had the mental health notes where it was recorded by the psychiatrist that she had no mental illness.

On the POS form the nurse also recorded drug and alcohol misuse. Did you speak to Yvonne about those?

I didn't discuss it because she'd already been on remand since the 9th December.

On the present risk indicators, the nurse has recorded a positive for 'talks of suicide'. Did you speak to Yvonne about that?

I didn't. I go on the overall, how she came across. She'd got a sentence that was less than she'd expected and she wasn't that upset that she didn't feel she couldn't cope until the New Year to see the psychologist. She was quite happy to wait for that, so she was thinking forwardly and she said that she'd be calm if she was moved out of the block from the beast. And the psychologist had seen her two weeks before and had said that he didn't think she would harm herself and the previous psychiatrist assessment recorded personality disorder rather than depressed.

If you had been made aware that the attempted hanging was in fact two years ago and not six years ago, would you have gone into that with Yvonne?

I suppose I would have done.

Had you known that the Leverndale admission was in February of that year and at that time Yvonne Gilmour was talking about killing herself, would you have gone into that with her?

I probably would have done, yes.

If you had known that Yvonne Gilmour told the nurse the night before that she had some suicidal thoughts while she'd been in Cornton Vale, would you have explored that with her?

I probably would have done. I can only assess her on how she is when she comes through the door that morning, what she felt like the night before may be completely different but you've got to assess them on how they are when they come through the door that day and take into account any further information that is available.

I appreciate that but it seems clear that you were not given this information by the nurse who say her the night before?

Correct.

What difference would that information have made to you the next day?

I really can't tell you. I might have asked more about it. I mean you've got to come back to the fact that I had an extremely angry young woman in the room with me, who I thought was going to attack the nurse in the room with me. She didn't give the impression of someone who was suicidal, it was someone who was much more positive rather than suicidal.

You mean your thinking that she was positive was because she's telling you that she's going to fucking murder someone?

Yes.

In order to carry out a proper assessment of Yvonne Gilmour, Doctor, you should have asked her about those previous risk indicators that were present on the form?

Sorry, are you telling me?

Well, I'm putting it to you that that's what you should have done?

She had already been in the prison for two or three weeks and she was just being admitted as a technical admission.

Irrespective of that, Doctor, you should have asked her more about these previous risk indicators that were shown on her form if you were carrying out a proper assessment. That is what you should have done?

If that's what you tell me.

What is your position on that?

Well I have never been trained in the Prevention of Suicide strategy.

Yes, because you were actually due to have your training on the

POS strategy in January of 1997. That is when you were booked for it wasn't it?

Correct.

And remind me of how long you had been carrying out the duties of a medical officer at the prison?

Since July 1989.

And during that period you had not had training on the operation of the POS strategy. Is that correct?

No, I hadn't.

And you were due to have training in January but in fact you finished the Prison Service on the 31st December?

Correct...

You have told us of your experience with psychiatric patients and you think that you have seen a significant number of patients who may have suicidal tendencies or expressed them?

Yes.

A doctor of your experience in this situation, does intuition have any part to play?

I think it has a large part to play. It is the whole way a person comes across and whether you feel they are hiding something or not. Very difficult to explain. We all have intuition about various things,

Is it a skill?

I think it is partly a skill. It is partly based on previous experience. You may not have anything tangible that you can say why you are worried for a particular patient. You just have the feeling, there is something not quite adding up. You feel that something is going to go wrong. Not everything adds up and you can't quite put your finger on why things don't add up but you have that intuition instilled.

I think you said that you had other prisoners to examine who were psychiatrically disturbed that morning?

Yes, about six. Three were awaiting psychiatric hospital placement and we were trying to get them out over the holiday period.

Its seems from your notes that you were reasonably secure in your assessment of Yvonne Gilmour on the morning of 24th December?

Yes, I felt that she was quite happy. She was the last person I thought would have done anything as I saw her that day.[134]

MEDICAL ADVISOR (SCOTTISH PRISON SERVICE)

It doesn't necessarily follow that an inmate will unburden herself in response to sympathetic questioning, is that right?

That is correct, just as they may not, for example, tell us about previous incidents.

Indeed. And there is a risk that they may play down their depressive symptoms, for example, for fear of being put on suicide supervision?

That is correct, yes.

So does that mean then that that kind of holistic approach, if I can put it that way, will never in its own right be a complete answer to the question of how one should assess suicide risk?

You cannot base your judgement purely on the answers you receive. You have to always have in mind somebody may be being evasive.

There is the prospect that an experienced clinician will be able to see through an attempt to disguise symptoms, is that fair?

I think that's a fair assessment.

But there is also a risk that they will be, in a sense, fooled by the prisoners...?

Yes, I mean the most skilled physician in the world may be fooled by anyone. Any one of us may be fooled by what somebody says.[135]

INMATE (48 YEARS OLD)

The day after Yvonne came into our block I was at a class in our sitting room. We were being shown slides by one of the prison staff about bullying in the prison. It was all about what to do if you were being bullied. It had already started when

Yvonne came in. The slide show was part of your induction and if you'd seen it before you didn't have to attend but I don't know if Yvonne had already saw it or not. Anyway she came in and sat down on the couch beside one of the lassies. All of a sudden she stood up, walked into the middle of the floor, looked at the slides for a couple of minutes and then turned and marched out of the room banging the door behind her. She seemed very upset about something. The slides showed pictures of prisoners assaulting other prisoners. Maybe that's what upset her. I really don't know.

I saw her again that day when she was being moved to Bravo. She seemed quite happy and was laughing and joking. Bravo Block is where all the young ones want to go because it's all hustle and bustle, whereas Sierra is very quiet. I was in Bravo for three weeks the last time and it was a bit too noisy and boisterous for me.[136]

PRISON OFFICER

There are only 14 spaces in the induction block and on occasion some people go straight through to the mainstream prison system. Obviously if someone has been in and out of prison on a number of occasions as in the case of Yvonne Gilmour, then they do not require to go through the full induction course and they can, with their consent, immediately be included into the mainstream of the prison. We give general information of prison life and services available, show videos on health issues, basic welfare, etc. The length of the stay for each prisoner depends on how long they are imprisoned. If their sentence is short, for example, for non-payment of a fine, then they are moved to the mainstream fairly quickly. If they have been through the induction course in the previous six months, they go through quickly. Anyone up to 12 months sentence, which we consider to be short, will probably get 3-5 days in induction, anyone with a sentence of more than one year stays about 14 days.

Yvonne approached me and asked when she was being transferred to Bravo. My colleague and I had already gone down the list of new inmates and Yvonne was one we had earmarked to move though to the mainstream very quickly but we hadn't told her before she approached us about 4pm on the Tuesday. Yvonne was very keen to move and sat blethering to me along with three or four other prisoners. She was ecstatic about going to Bravo, really happy. I was actually quite relieved that she was keen to move. We were a bit pressed for space and it's better for us if people are keen to move. Some, however, are more settled in the smaller environment of the induction unit. We had earmarked three in all to move on that day and one of them didn't want to move. There was also the question of the prisoner Yvonne had threatened to have a go at. Sierra Unit is split in two, half is for induction and the other half is for a drugs unit and special suicide watch but due to shortage of space it had been used to hold convicted prisoners. I didn't want Yvonne and this other prisoner to bump into each other.[137]

PRISON OFFICER

Yvonne was admitted to Bravo Block on Tuesday 24th December when I was on duty. She arrived about 7pm from Sierra. I knew Yvonne from previous sentences and I chatted to her. She seemed in good spirits, quite hyperactive. She knew quite a few girls on the block and she wandered around meeting different girls she had probably met in prison before. She went away for medication and she was away quite a while and then she went away to visit someone else and then about 20 to 9 I placed her in her room for lock-up. She wasn't sharing. The only thing she was concerned about was that she didn't have a set of drawers for her clothes. I told her this would be attended to by the daytime staff the next day as there was no time to do it that night. She seemed quite happy with this.[138]

INMATE (34 YEARS OLD)

I saw Yvonne not long after she came over from Sierra. We had a joke about her running around carrying a lamp. I saw her again just before she was getting locked up and I was going up to my unit and she was running down the stairs and she was asking me how I was and that and I said I was great and she was laughing but she just said, 'I'll see you in the morning, scouse'. I was carrying a wee heart I'd took off the Christmas tree and she was laughing and squeezing the wee heart and that, she said, 'You're mad, scouser, I'll see you in the morning'.[139]

INMATE (33 YEARS OLD)

Yvonne wisnae her usual cheery self that night she came over from Sierra. She wis different, no' exactly angry, but jist different. Ah jist took it, it wis because she got a sentence. Then ah asked her, ah says, when I fund oot she wis in Sierra for the night before, I says to her how did ye no' stay over there 'cause Cathy's o'er there, she wis put back on a Rule, an' she jist says she fell oot wi' her or finished wi' her, 'cause she wis a cheatin' cow.[140]

INMATE (19 YEARS OLD)

Well, Yvonne came into Bravo Block that night. It wis ma room-mate Sandra that met her. Yvonne wis gay, right, an' she wis tryin' to get an early relationship wi Sandra. But Sandra didnae want tae so when Yvonne tried to come on tae Sandra, Sandra backed aff, she didnae want tae get intae that kind o' thing wae wummen. An' Yvonne wis 'Who's Sandra gawn wi' hersel' though?' and that'd be because she pushed her away. But I think she wis cryin' for help but we had to push her away in case we got lesbians, dae ye know whit ah mean? Yvonne came up tae Sandra's room an' ah wis there as well. Me an' Sandra wur best pals, we still are. It must've been half-seven, quarter to eight when Yvonne came in. She wis wi' us then aw night tae yon time. She wis comin' aff methadone an aw. She wis strung oot tae the dogs, she wis bad. Ah kept lookin' at her tattoo, she's got a big wummen on her right arm. A big wummen wi' suspenders an' that, right. We were jist talkin' in oor room then we went alang tae the pool room. We were jist playin' pool an' she kept saying 'Ah'm dreadin' goin' in this room' an' aw that. She wis cryin' for help. Yvonne wis in a depressin' mood.

Sandra's bed's there when yi walk intae the room, her bed's there, right, an' the bunk was there. Yvonnne wis leanin' on the bunk an' talkin' tae me an' Sandra. An' then she says to Sandra 'C'mere a minute' an' went ootside the door. An' ah wis thinkin' she's gonnae try an' fire intae Sandra. Sandra's like 'Naw, naw.' Ah heard her sayin' 'Naw, naw' ootside. They've came back in the room. Ah've went 'C'mon we'll go alang the pool room' 'cause Sandra wis kinda daen that wi' her eyes to us as if she wis askin' me oot the room, askin' whatever, right. Ah've asked her tae go alang the pool room, she says 'Naw'. Ah says 'C'mon', she says 'Naw', an' Sandra went 'C'mon' so she's flew up since it wis Sandra that asked her. We went alang tae the pool room. Ah mean, Yvonne wis mair pleased tae see Sandra than she wis wi' me, 'cause Sandra is a good, good pal, do you know what ah mean. I think she's brilliant, Sandra. Ah liked her as a pal an' that, nothing else, do you know what ah mean. Well, ah played pool, ah've took the hi-fi oot Unit 4 an' took it up tae Unit 2 pool room. Unit 2 they've got a couch an' that, an' a big pool room an' a sittin' room. An' ah had the music up, aw blastin' an' that an' Marilyn she's gawn 'Turn that doon a bit, ah'm still comin' aff the methadone.' Ah turned the music an' that doon, jist played pool, an' Yvonne kept beatin' me an' Sandra, so she wis jist slaggin' us an' aw that an' we went back alang tae Unit 4. Sandra put the kettle on tae make her tea an' doon the stair, Units 1,3 an' 5 an' 6 get locked up at half-eight, it's only the lassies aff observations that get locked up at quarter tae nine. So me an' Sandra were oot till quarter tae nine but they shouted room time so it wis half-eight. Me an' Sandra wur gettin' ready for oor room, makin' tea an' that, when they shouted room time. Yvonne went 'That's room time already. Right, I'll catch ye in the mornin', lassies.' Ah says, 'We'll see yi at the windae.' She kept sayin 'Ah don't want tae go intae this room' an' then she went doon the stair an' that wis the last we seen o' her.[141]

INMATE (19 YEARS OLD)

After we played pool, an' we were makin' wur tea, Yvonne wis in the sittin' room shouting at Lesley Cochrane. Sandra an' me went in and Sandra pulled Yvonne away. Yvonne didn't like the crime Lesley had committed and she thought Lesley was too friendly with her girlfriend Cathy Preston. She thought she was always running to Cathy.[142]

INMATE (33 YEARS OLD)

So it was when you were queuing for the phone at 6.50pm on the 24th December that you spoke to Yvonne Gilmour?

Uh huh. She'd just come over from another block and I chatted to her a bit. She wisnae her usual self. She wis quiet, a bit paranoid, no' very, just a bit but she wis coming aff the drugs. She was just fidgety, moving about, looking about her.

What was she paranoid about?

I don't know. She asked me if I knew anything about her girlfriend Cathy Preston and another lassie. Ye ken, she was going out wi Cathy an' like she'd been told that Cathy was messing about wi' another lassie on the block. I knew about it but I said I didnae know nothing.

Did she say anything about how she felt about being in Bravo Block?

She said she'd told the staff that she wanted moved on to Bravo from Sierra. She says that she'd told them that she'd gonna be bungy jumping if they didnae move her out the block.

Was there anyone else there when she said this to you?

Aye, a couple of lassies.

Did she actually use the expression 'bungy jumping'?

Uh huh.

Are you quite sure about that?

Aye. I've been in the jail for four years and everybody uses bungy jumping, even me.

In your police statement, could it be that you said that Yvonne's remarks to the prison officers was 'I'll be swinging from the bars if they don't move me'?

Uh huh.

So it wasn't bungy jumping then?

Uh huh.

It means the same thing but it's different words, is that fair?

Uh huh.

Did you see her again that evening?

Aye. She was arguing wi' an inmate called Lesley Cochrane and this other lassie Sandra had to pull her off Lesley. She was pulling her out of Lesley's room. Sandra says, Just leave it, she's no' worth it.

Now did you witness this yourself or did you hear about it later? In your police statement, you said...

Maybe, I don't know, I cannae remember, ma heid's all messed up. I've been in there every death. But I'm positive I saw it, I heard, I don't know, I'm all mixed up.[143]

INMATE (19 YEARS OLD)

It wis Christmas Eve an' we wur making the tea and Yvonne wis in the living room waitin'. It wis jist before she got locked up fur the night. She wis arguin' wi' Lesley Cochrane sayin' 'Whit are ye daen wi' ma pal' an' aw that.' But she wisnae botherin', she wanted tae batter Lesley because she wis a beast, classed as a beast. An' using Cathy Preston as an excuse, because Cathy Preston wisnae even gawn wi' Yvonne. They wir only writin' letters tae each other fae block tae block. Sandra pulled Yvonne away fae her an' says 'Jist leave it, c'mon an' have a cup o' tea.' But they got shouted for room time an' Yvonne had tae go.[144]

INMATE (17 YEARS OLD)

On Christmas Eve of last year you were an inmate in Bravo Block in Cornton Vale?

Yes.

In the course of that evening, the 24th December, did you meet another inmate called Yvonne Gilmour?

Yes. It was just after she got shifted over from Sierra, about half past eight.

Was that the first time you had met her?
No, I'd met her before on my last sentence.

What sort of mood was Yvonne in that night?
A bad mood.

What about?
She was talking to me about her girlfriend Cathy Preston.

What was she saying?
She was asking me if I had a relationship with her.

With Cathy Preston?
Yes.

And was she angry towards you?
Yes.

Was she aggressive?
Yes.

Did she shout at you?
Yes.

Did she swear?
Yes.

Did she threaten you?
No.

Were there other inmates present?
Yes.

How did the incident end up?
Another inmate, Sandra, came in at the end, that was when Yvonne was just about to walk out and she asked Yvonne what was happening. Yvonne told Sandra that someone had told her that her girlfriend was having a relationship, that I was having a relationship with Yvonne's girlfriend.

And what did Sandra do?
She more or less pulled Yvonne out of the sitting room.

You mean physically pulled her?
No, just says, 'Come on, Yvonne.' I cannae mind the exact words but she took her arm and took her out of the sitting room.

Now let me get this clear. You are saying that you think the reason that Yvonne Gilmour was getting on to you was because somebody had told her you were having a relationship with Cathy Preston?

Yes.

Did you know that at the time Yvonne was having a go at you?

No' until she says it.

Can you remember what her exact words were?

'Did you nick my fuckin' bird?'[145]

INMATE (19 YEARS OLD)

Right after lock-up ah went tae ma windae. Ah could see Yvonne's windae frae ma room. It wis across frae ma windae. Her curtains were open a wee bit an' she wis sittin' on the bed. Ye see, there's this lassie, right, Lesley Cochrane, she's in fir daen somethin' bad, naebody likes her, but she's always doon, dead depressed, so we always watch her, so we dae, she's aff obs. She's on a long sentence an' had just lost her appeal. She gets a lot of strife from people because of what she is, right, and what she'd done. She's had a few doings in there. Sandra wis at her windae tae an' we both shouted across to Lesley who wis in the room right above Yvonne's tae see if she wis okay. Lesley came tae her windae as well an' we all had a bit of a laugh talkin' aboot Christmas presents an' things. Sandra wis talkin' away tae Yvonne an' ah wis shoutin' at Lesley an' wisin' her up, something daft, right. Yvonne wis laughin' cause o' her underwear, she showed us them fae the windae, an' she wis laughin'. She wis tellin' us that she wis in Sierra Block afore she came ower that night. An' she telt me she didnae get any bra an' so they sent her a bra. She telt us that she'd said tae the staff over there in Sierra, if they don't send her oot of Sierra, she's gonnae dae somethin' tae hersel'. She said she had told the officers 'If you don't get me out of here, I'm going to bungy jump from the bars.'

Anyway then someone put the ghetto blasters on an' there

wis the Oasis song *Champagne Supernova* an' *Uncomfortably Numb*[146] by Pink Floyd, an' the music was goin' dead loud and the conversation wis drowned oot. Yvonne kept gawn in and oot and fidgeting aboot wi her curtains an' she said 'Who's playin' that music?' Ah went 'Frannie' It was a song *Uncomfortably Numb*, right, Pink Floyd. Everybody likes it. Ah went 'Frannie's playin' it'. She went 'That's awright. Turn it up, Frannie' and went back in an' shut her windae, put her light oot, put it back on. Ah stayed at the windae an' ah sang *Uncomfortably Numb*.[147]

Hello.
Is there anybody there?
Just nod if you can hear me
Is there anyone at home?

Come on, now.
I hear you're feeling down
Well, I can ease your pain
Get you on your feet again

Relax.
I need some information first
Just the basic facts:
Can you show me where it hurts?

There is no pain, you are receding,
A distant ship's smoke on the horizon.
You are only coming through in waves
Your lips move but I can't hear what you're sayin'.
When I was a child I had a fever.
My hands felt just like two balloons.
Now I got that feeling once again.
I can't explain, you would not understand.
This is not how I am.
I have become comfortably numb.

Ok.

Just a little pinprick
There'll be more – Aaaaaahhhhh!
But you may feel a little sick.

Can you stand up?
I do believe it's working. Good.
That'll keep you going for the show
Come on, it's time to go.

When I was a child I caught a fleeting glimpse
Out of the corner of my eye.
I turned to look but it was gone.
I cannot put my finger on it now.
The child is grown, the dream is gone.
I have become comfortably numb.[148]

INMATE (19 YEARS OLD)

So after you were in your cell, after lock-up, you were speaking to Yvonne while she was in her cell?

Uhuh.

What were you speaking about?

Underwear an' aw that.

Underwear. What sort of mood did Yvonne seem to be in at that time?

She's stressed oot, she's pure sweats and cauld sweats, an' aw pains, she's strung right oot.

But speaking to her one to one, what sort of mood did she seem to be in?

We telt her tae go tae the doctor's an' she said naw. She wis awright but when yir strung oot it's jist a big itch ye've got on. Tae yerself.

You're describing what you thought about her but what I'm interested in is...?

Ah'm describin' what everybody goes through, what a druggie goes through.

Tell me what mood she seemed to be in when you were

speaking to her from the window of your cell?

She was laughin' 'cause o' her underwear, she showed us them fae the windae, an' she wis laughin'.

How long after her being locked up was this conversation taking place?

How long efter we wur locked up?

Yes.

Ages.

Was this...?

Back o' ten we wur still talkin'.

How much time did you spend speaking to her at that time?

Ah got locked up aboot quarter tae nine, so ten, half-ten.

Were there other inmates at their windows in the block?

A few, aye.

So you were talkin' to other people apart from Yvonne, is that fair?

Aye. The music wis goin' dead loud, Pink Floyd an' that. Yvonne kept gawn in an' comin' back oot, an' fidgeting aboot wae her curtains. But we didnae think anything o' it right, an' she came back tae her windae 'Who's playing that music?' as if she wis in a bad mood. Ah went 'Frannie'. It wis *Uncomfortably Numb* by Pink Floyd. Ah went 'Frannie's playin' it' and she went 'That's awright' an' went back in an' shut her windae, put her light oot, put it back on, came tae the windae, kept gawn back in puttin' her light oot. She kept gawn in an' oot o' the windae to put her light on an' aff, fidgetin' aboot wae her curtains. But sees, ah look above, tae Lesley Cochrane's room above Yvonne and somebody else, Christine something, she works in the hairdresser's, she's in another block noo, she did the decoration for her windae an' that's whit we thought was on Yvonne's windae.

Well, let's take that bit by bit. You said a moment ago that the last time you spoke to Yvonne was about half past ten?

Well, we wur talking right up tae aboot half-ten, when she kept gawn in an' oot, in an' oot.

So up to about 10.30?

An' wan o' the officers said the next day tae us that she wis writin' a letter tae her ma but we don't know whit she wis doin' in her room.

Could we stick to what you remember from what you yourself heard or saw? What did you speak to her about around 10.30 that night?

She wis tellin' us that she wis in Sierra Block afore she came ower that night. An' she telt me she didnae get any bra an' she wis gawn like this an' like that tae hersel' so they sent her a bra.

Well, we'll come back to that but as far as the evening you were speaking to her at the window, do you remember what you talked to her about?

Jist havin' a conversation wae somebody, huv ah got tae take notes o' it?

I quite undersatnd. You mentioned an incident when she came to the window and asked for music to be turned down?

Naw, she said 'Who's playin' that music?'

Who's playing music, sorry. When did that happen roughly?

Don't know.

You mentioned also something about a decoration hanging from the window above Yvonne's cell?

Aye.

Was that dangling down from the window?

The windae, aye, the middle bar.

Thank you. Then you mentioned seeing something at, or about, the window of Yvonne's cell, is that right?

Aye.

What did you actually see?

It wisnae the windae, it wis outside, jist sort o' hinging doon. She kept fidgeting aboot wae her curtains so she must've, ah'm jist assumin' that she tied it roon, when ah seen her fidgetin' at the curtains.

Was this on the inside of her window, or the outside?

In her room she was daen it. She's here an' we're there, we're watching there an' she's at this side o' her curtain.

Was this before you last spoke to her or after you last spoke to her?

We'd spoke to her efter she'd hanged that up. We'd jist count it as decorations, we didnae know, ken whit ah mean.

Now you mentioned a conversation about Sierra Block. When did that conversation take place?

At the windae.

So that's the same evening?

Uhuh.

And can you tell us exactly what she said about Sierra Block?

She said that she'd said to the staff if they don't get her oot of Sierra she's gawn to dae somethin' tae hersel. An' they sent her to Bravo an' she still done it, so it's been a cry for help. But there's never any help fir ye in there.

You say that Yvonne told you that when she was in Sierra Block she'd said to the staff if they don't move her, she would what?

Harm herself. 'Bungy jump' was the word she used.

'Bungy jump'?

Aye.

Is that a phrase that you'd heard used before in prison?

Ah wis fightin' a lassie because if ah hear anybody talkin' aboot they're gonnae hing theirsel, ah go tae the officers an aw that because ah couldnae allow a person tae dae that.

And Yvonne told you that she told the prison officers in Sierra that she was going to 'bungy jump'?

Aye. Ma pal Sandra wis over there in Sierra talking tae a Q worker an' she wis shoutin' and bawlin' at aw the officers.

How did this...?

That night an aw, she went intae ma sittin' room when we came back fae the pool room, she went intae Unit 4 sitting-room 'cause wee Lesley Cochrane goes 'Fast as a beast fae Greenock' fir the lassie anyway, right, she wis gonnae batter her because she nipped Cathy Preston, an' Lesley went wae Cathy Preston an' Yvonne used to go wae her. She wis writin' letters tae her.

I want to try and keep track of this. You've now moved away from the conversation at the window, all right. The simplest way is for you just to take it bit by bit and listen to my questions and just...?

Ah jist want it done.

I understand that. Hopefully, I won't be too much longer with you. This conversation about the bungy jump...?

Aye, ah cannae understand if she'd got there to Bravo Block where she wanted, she got what she wanted. So why did she dae it anyway. For people tae say that, ye take them serious, in ma block anyway, in Bravo Block an' Papa. Papa's that privileged ye get yer ain key an' aw that.

Were you worried about Yvonne at the time she mentioned the 'bungy jump'?

Naw, ah wis worried aboot Lesley. 'Cause Lesley wis depressed because Yvonne wis gonnae batter her, she picked on her constantly 'cause o' what she's in prison fir.

Now I don't want to put words into your mouth about this so please correct me if I'm not right about this, but I do take it from what you've said that when Yvonne told you about this 'bungy jumping' conversation, it didn't make you think at the time that you were worried about Yvonne doing something to herself?

'Cause that happened in Sierra, she wanted tae get oot tae Bravo, a lot of people jist say that tae get shifted. But they dinnae usually get shifted, they usually get shifted tae Triple S.

You're explaining reasons rather than answering my questions...

That's what happens, that's prison life.

Can I try the question again because I want to be clear about what your position on this is?

Ah didnae believe that she wis serious, ah believe she said it an' aw that, but it jist didnae take note in my head that she would've done that to hersel. If ah thought she'd a done that then a'd a reported it, aye. Look, this is the third one ah've been there fur. It wis Angela's death that really affected me, the others...

Did you think that night that Yvonne might do anything to harm herself?

Ah said naw.[149]

PRISON OFFICER

I was on night shift on Christmas Eve. The late shift staff said that all of the girls had had a great time, they were all in good spirits and there was nothing to report. They said it should be a good night. But it was a terrible night. I was observing 15 prisoners out of 52 in Bravo that night, in Units 1, 3 and 5. That's the three ground floor units. As soon as the late shift staff left, I started off doing my checks, my final checks and my security checks. I checked the units which were closed off, like 7 and 8. I checked the kitchens and sitting rooms for fire and security. I went upstairs to Unit 8 and checked that, went through to Unit 6, done the same checks and then I came down to Unit 5. I started to check the girls in Unit 5, spoke to them all, while I was also doing the checks in the toilets, making sure the windows and that were closed. I went into Unit 3 and all the girls were playing their radios. It was quite a happy night and they all seemed in good spirits. There was two or three that were hanging out their windows speaking to one another. I called to them to close their windows or they would be catching the cold, and for to tone down their radios. You know, it is better that they appeared to be in good spirits and didn't appear depressed, and I spoke to all the girls. Then I went up to Unit 4 and done my security checks and I came down to Unit 1 last and I checked room 4 first, room 5 and I crossed over to room 2 because the wee lassie was complaining that she wasn't on obs and could I stop observing her. I said I would get that checked out and I crossed over to room 6 which was Yvonne's room and I spoke to her. She was sitting at her bench. She had her head resting on her left arm and she was writing a letter. It was about five to ten, maybe ten, because it takes about 10 minutes to look in on all the girls. I said to Yvonne. 'Hi, how are you getting on?' She said something but she didn't look at me and then I says to her, 'Well, come on, Yvonne, let's see you' and she turned round and just gave me a little half smile. I says, 'How are you?' and she says 'Fine' and I says 'Good night, hen.' She wasn't sharing. In fact, there wasn't anybody sharing in Bravo that night.

The next time I went to Yvonne's room I know for sure what time it was because I got asked by a prisoner about the time, because there was still quite a few of them awake and they were still playing their radios too loud and I asked them to turn it down, and a prisoner asked me what time is it, and I looked at my watch, it was five to eleven. I checked another one after that girl, turned the corner to go into Unit 1. I checked room 4, room 5, I went over to room 2, told the prisoner in room 2 that she wasn't on observes and then she changed her mind and said, 'Och well, you can still watch me if you want.' I says, 'Right'. By this time, it must have been about six minutes past eleven. I crossed over to room 6, Yvonne's room, and as I went to put the light on I had a look through the spy, Yvonne was hanging from her window.[150]

INMATE (19 YEARS OLD)

Ah went tae ma bed an' fell asleep an' the next thing ah know Sandra wis shoutin' at the top of her voice, calling oot the names of everybody in the block. Ah looked oot the windae an' ah saw Yvonne's light on. The curtains were now shut tight together. Ah never thought it wis Yvonne. People were shoutin' 'It's Tessy'. Later we heard Code Blue on the prison radios an' we knew it wis a hangin'. Everyone knows whit Code Blue means. Ah wis really upset after that. Ah saw an officer runnin' across the yard tae bring the ambulance people in an' ah saw the ambulance. An officer told us tae close wur curtains and shut the windaes. It wis then ah smashed up ma cell. It wis too much. Ah had enough wi Angela's suicide. She hung herself too an' that wis jist a few months back. [151]

PRISON OFFICER

I radioed the code for hanging which is Code Blue, three times to get assistance, and at the same time, I was aware that I had a nurse sitting along in Unit 3 and also a male officer. He was guarding a prisoner whose door had to be left open all night as she was in the habit of taking fits, so she had to be observed all night. After I put in the second call, I called out for the nurse and the officer at the top of ma lungs.. The patrol also ended up coming at the same time so everybody was there in seconds. It all took only a few seconds. I know that everything appeared to be going in slow motion but it's being done. The outside patrol only happened to be outside the block when the call came through so they really had to run about ten or twenty yards to get to the block, so maybe it took about three seconds, four seconds, but I got the calls through on the radio, looked round, there's going to be help, and go for my sealed pack to get the key out to unlock the cell door. It was quicker to use the key in the pack than get control to open the door. My hands were shaking and I couldn't get the pack open. You're actually supposed to use the little knife attached to open the pack but time was off the essence and I was trying to open it with my fingers but I was shaking too much. The patrol officer came running up and grabbed the pack from me. She burst it open and got the key out. The nurse was standing at the door waiting to get in with another female officer. We handed them the key and they opened the door and they went right in and started to take Yvonne's weight. I went in, I jumped on the bed and I tried to cut down the noose using the knife from the sealed pack. But it didn't work very well and the other officer ran and got a pair of scissors that were handy in the office. It took only a few seconds and the nurse and two members of staff were holding Yvonne up. She had a piece of sheeting that she had torn from her bed, she had it round her neck. It was attached to the top bar at the window and it was wound round three times and I know that because when I was trying to cut the ligature I could see that the sheet went round the bar three times. It then went down to her neck and it was round her neck twice with the knot on the left. I can't remember anything about her face or what she was wearing or anything. I've blanked it out. I've blanked out her face. I didn't think she was dead. I thought they were going to be able to save her, to resuscitate her. I thought that maybe she had only just done it, just before I was due to appear at her cell and I was just hoping she would be alive. When they were getting the body down, I was kind of trapped in the room at the back. I didn't want to interfere with what they were doing. I heard someone asking if they had got a pulse. They were asking each other, have you got a pulse, have you got a pulse.

The ambulance arrived quite quickly.[152]

INMATE (33 YEARS OLD)

We seen an ambulance. Its siren wis screaming. I looked oot the windae and the ambulance men came oot o' the ambulance and they went in the side door underneath ma windae, an' ah could see in Unit 1, an' all the staff were runnin' aboot an ah heard Code Blue gettin' mentioned, somebody had tried to commit suicide, so we were shouting at the ambulance men hurry up, hurry up, an' we were swearing as well an' we seen the ambulance men comin' oot withoot anybody on the streetcher so we knew then somebody wis dead, so we all jist started screaming and the officers eventually came round and put us, three of us, into Sandra's room and later we found oot who it wis 'cause we seen the flashes of the camera in Yvonne's room.[153]

AGENCY NURSE, CORNTON VALE

Can you please describe the appearance of the young lady as you first entered the cell?

Well, she was hanging there with the noose round her neck, the eyes were open in slight slits and there was a slight protrusion of the tongue. The other thing I noticed was that the toes of her left foot were still in contact with the chair, which was placed in front of the radiator underneath the bars. We then cut her down.

Did you notice anything about her complexion?

Slightly pallid, not particularly cyanosed.

Was there any sign of consciousness or life?

No.

How long did the resuscitation attempt last?

It would be a guess, about ten minutes.

At any stage was there any indication of life?

Never.[154]

MEDICAL DOCTOR

I was at a Christmas Eve church service when my bleeper activated. I got a message to got to Cornton Vale prison. It was approximately 11.15. The church is very close to the prison so it was about twenty past eleven at the latest when I entered the cell. The ambulance personnel were attempting resuscitation. There was an oxygen mask on, cardiac massage was being attempted and artificial respiration through the pulmonary bag. They had ECG leads on as well. The ambulance personnel said they had been there for some minutes and what I saw on the ECG was what they had seen the first time they put it on. There had been no success at all. I noted while they were working that the ECG had a flat trace, i.e. there was no electrical stimulation at all. I noticed that her pupils were fixed and dilated but I allowed them to continue with their attempt at resuscitation for another few minutes just so that I could see what was happening, but after, I mean, I honestly don't know how many more minutes, I said 'Look, this is a waste of time. This is gone.' So she had a formal examination that there was no heart signs, no breath signs, her pupils were fixed and dilated. She had a significant ligature mark around her neck extending from behind the right ear down and across round to the left hand side and it would probably be about 11.25 that I pronounced life extinct.[155]

INMATE (19 YEARS OLD)

Later they put me in a cell wae Sandra an' she told me it wis Yvonne. Ah never knew Yvonne to talk aboot killin' herself or anything like that. When we were in the pool room together an' she telt us when she wis in Sierra the day before she'd told the officers there, 'If youse don't get me out of this block you'll find me on the bars takin' a bungee jump.' But she probably just said it. She wisnae the type. An' anyway, she got oot of Sierra like she wanted.

If ye ask me, it wis the drugs that did it. Ah mean, comin' off them. They give you valium and dihydrocodeine to help you but it's no' enough if ye're comin' off methadone.[156]

CAROLANN

On Tuesday 24th December I was up at Michelle's in the afternoon and got back about 8 o'clock. My boyfriend told me that Yvonne had phoned about 4 o'clock and would phone back. He said she was fine and was having a laugh and a joke with him.

MICHELLE

About half past two on Christmas morning, well still Christmas Eve really, my door went. I admit I wasn't going to answer it because I'd had a break-in a number of months before that but I just answered it with it being Christmas Eve. I thought it could be somebody chancing their luck, Christmas presents or what have you and I answered the door and the police were there. They asked who I was and I told them and they said 'Can we come in?' and then we went into the living room and they says something about Yvonne and I says, 'She's in the jail', and they says, 'We're sorry but she has passed away' and I says, 'No,

Yvonne

A young Yvonne (centre) meets Santa

Yvonne (centre) with her sisters

Yvonne (right) and a friend at a wedding

Yvonne (damaged print)

Yvonne (left) with sister Michelle

she's in the jail.' I can't think of any reason why Yvonne would do what she did. She always seemed too strong to do something like that. Maybe it was because she was coming off drugs and she thought she couldn't handle it.

CAROLANN

At the back of 3a.m. on Wednesday, 25th December, my dad phoned me at home and told me that Yvonne had passed away at the prison. He didn't say how she had died but I later learned that she had hung herself in her cell.

The only thing that I can think of as to why Yvonne took her life is that she thought that she would always be in and out of prison. I know that she tried hard to beat the drugs but I think it was just too hard for her. I also believe that Yvonne had nothing of her own like Michelle and I had. We have children, Yvonne had none. It was basically that she wanted to be at peace with herself.

YVONNE

I'm really sorry to everyone but I really can't wake up in the morning without my family. People may think I've taken the easy way out but please believe me this is the hardest thing I've ever had to do. I don't know which way to go, so I guess this is the easy way. I love my family so much so please don't let them know I killed myself on Christmas Day. I'm sorry for everything I've done but I really can't cope and I know if I got out my life would not change. Drugs have taken over me and if I let it it always will, but I can't. Please tell my girlfriend, Cathy Preston, I am so sorry but I wanted to be with her but youse fucked that up. So thanks a lot and I hope youse all have a great Christmas.

Y. Gilmour

RIP[157]

Epilogue

Determination by John Joseph Maguire, Queen's Counsel, Sheriff Principal of the Sheriffdom of Tayside Central and Fife in Fatal Accident Inquiry into the deaths of Angela Bollan, Denise Anne Devine and Yvonne Gilmour, 18th November 1997.

It is noteworthy that there are a number of areas in which the Scottish Prison Service has responded to the recent suicides.[158]

GOVERNOR

What happened when I first went to Cornton Vale is obviously I was concerned about the suicide history so I began to do some research of my own and subsequently I had a colleague have a look at all the papers that he could possibly find in relation to all the deaths and to go through each of them to see if there were any lessons that we might learn from them.

What happens after any kind of incident is that staff on duty have an opportunity to sit down together and go over their experience of what happened. That gives them an opportunity not only to be debriefed because involvement in any kind of incident can be a very traumatic experience, but it gives us a chance to see whether any of the systems and processes that took place when an incident happens are as good as they might be. A group or individual will go through the papers and see whether there are any lessons to be learned.

We gathered all the papers together and produced a document which helped us to see whether there were any common threads relating to all of the six deaths and the circumstances surrounding them. I mean, clearly each is subject to a Fatal Accident Inquiry but there's a great deal that we wanted to know about the anatomy of each of them as well as to see if there were any lessons that we could quickly learn.

Since I have been Governor, inmates spend more time out of their cells in association with other people, about two hours a day more, longer at the weekends. In the remand unit there were previously a supervisor and five officers. There is now a complement of supervisors and six officers, which means that women are out of their cell much more often than was possible previously, and it's a big difference at the weekend. It's now routine that the women get out at the weekend. If we have staff shortages for any reason, staff will be concentrated in the remand unit. They will be given priority in terms of full staffing.

We no longer have a central canteen. We have a canteen in each of the blocks in order to have a greater accessibility to the canteen. Officers still have to leave the remand block to cover remand visits and for escort duties but we try to minimise the number of out-of-block activities that our residential staff have to be involved in.

There has been an increase in the amount of educational opportunities available to remand prisoners, about ten hours a week. We've also changed the nature of the educational opportunities on offer, because by and large the women tend to have very poor levels of concentration, they tend to be a bit lethargic and not very interested. So instead of offering numeracy and literacy we now offer practical craft work and art and something which is of more interest and which they can do in association together. Attendance at the classes is optional.

All the internal security bars have been removed from the windows in the remand block and I intend to ask for resources to put the bars on the outside of all windows in Cornton Vale. A lot of self-harm behaviour is impulsive and opportunistic, that's our experience in the prison, in the Prison Service, and therefore, a very practical step is to take one of the most obvious ligature points out of the cells and put them on the outside.

We had observation hatches put in all the doors in remand which means you can have direct contact with the prisoner, like a cigarette or something can be passed through. It is more than the observation hatch was. Officers can talk to the prisoners directly instead of speaking through a door.

There has been the suggestion of having televisions in cells but I think it might then be difficult to get the women to come out of the cells to associate with each other and there's the danger they might become even more isolated and solitary. I would be prepared to be proven wrong in that assumption and I would be prepared to look at a pilot study for Cornton Vale if that was felt to be appropriate.

We now have two telephones in remand instead of one.

We have three more nurses, registered mental nurses, which means that our complement of nurses is now thirteen.

We have an additional two psychiatric sessions a week, a session being half a day, which means we now have six sessions a week. One of the additional ones is taken up by a consultant psychiatrist who also has expertise in drug addiction and the other a consultant psychiatrist with special expertise in sex abuse.

There are plans to establish formal contact with outside agencies. The medical officer is setting up a system whereby he will be able to contact GP's more easily. We're also in discussion about a partnership with an organisation called Turning Point, which is a drugs charity. They are about to appoint a drugs worker to the Court of Glasgow, which is where the vast majority of our women come from. That person will link with a Turning Point addictions worker in Cornton Vale. Turning Point is very familiar with a lot of women who come to Cornton Vale, so that should help us far better to share information.

There are plans to recruit a trained addiction worker to work with us full-time and for intensive social work support sessions in respect of drug addiction.

We are planning a needs assessment for each admission and automatic urine testing would help us assess each incoming prisoner.

We have been making our documentation for induction and reception into remand more systematic. We are also planning a system whereby prisoner files are stored in reception so that reception staff can refer to them immediately. The files will then follow the prisoners to their blocks.

There have been measures taken to improve the quality of staff training, including the operation of the suicide prevention strategy. We have refresher courses for staff and also the Samaritans now come in to supplement that training in vulnerability recognition. [159]

Transcript of Proceedings in Fatal Accident Inquiry into the death of Angella Bollan and others, 23rd and 24th June 1997

†3rd December 1997

Sandra Brown's background was unfortunate. Some of her family members suffered from a disease for which there is no known cure. ... It is mercifully rare. ... Sandra was aware of the family history. Her mother had the disease. She said that her mother committed suicide. ... Although her doctor arranged appointments for her at a genetics clinic, Sandra failed to attend. She did not know whether or not she had the disease. Her father died when she was 8. Sandra was brought up by her sister. She refused to go to school and was eventually sent to a residential school. She had a child when she was 17. The boy was from an early age looked after by her sister. Because of her lifestyle it was felt that Sandra could not look after the child properly. She started abusing drugs at the age of 12 or 13. Her abuse involved heroin, methadone and dihydrocodeine and diazepam and temazepam. She was in touch with the Community Drug Problem Service in Edinburgh. She was admitted to the Accident and Emergency Department of Edinburgh Royal Infirmary following an overdose. ... She led a chaotic lifestyle.

She was no stranger to Cornton Vale, having been there in 1992 and 1993 and August 1997. She was admitted on 24 November 1997, sentenced to 6 months' imprisonment for assault. The charge had been reduced from attempted murder.

Sandra B. was seen by the Senior Medical Officer the next day. He was well versed in dealing with drug addictions. He found Sandra not overly communicative or forthcoming. ... She spoke about the disease. ... She said a brother had it and she felt a sister had it. She felt that she had it too. ... She had been counselled by a psychiatrist not to have any tests done. She was very much in control during the interview. She told the doctor: Don't worry. I won't commit suicide in your poxy jail. He formed the view that while her background risk factors were high she did not present as an imminent suicide risk. ... He put her on dihydrocodeine and diazepam and lomitol. He had her prescription checked with her GP.

The residential officers thought she fitted in well to the prison regime. She was not forthcoming to the officers. She could flare up easily and had done so in her earlier incarcerations... She did not have much time for male officers. She felt they had allowed a friend of hers to die. She discussed death with another prisoner. She felt that she had Huntingdon's Chorea. She said that she would never take her own life but would go to Holland and get someone to do it for her. She did not have many dealings with her family. She had no visits or mail. One prisoner said that she kept bringing the conversation and lectures to discussions about her friend's death. ... Nonetheless the impression I formed was of someone who was getting on with her life in prison.

On 3 December the meal was late in coming over. It did not arrive until after 4.30p.m. ... The locking up for 5.00p.m. which usually began by about 4.50p.m. was late because of the late arrival of the tea. The girls seemed to have been rushing about from their sitting rooms to their cells. An officer looked into Sandra's cell. He noticed that the sheet was not on the bed. He thought Sandra might be in the toilet. Another prisoner asked, 'Where is Sandra?' The officer went back to her room. He found her hanging from a ligature over the edge of the wardrobe.

It would appear that ... Sandra took the sheet from her bed and fixed up an elaborate mechanism to hang herself. ... She must have tied the sheet around the [coathanger] bar and then led it back and upwards through the gap and then over the side wall of the wardrobe where she tied it round her neck and suspended herself. From that point it would have taken her at most four minutes to die. Unconsciousness would have occurred much more quickly.[160]

Determination by John Joseph Maguire, Queen's Counsel, Sheriff Principal of the Sheriffdom of Tayside Central and Fife in Fatal Accident Inquiry into the death of Sandra Brown, 17th August 1998.

†4th July 1998

On 16th June Mary Cowan, was arrested for shoplifting and remanded in custody to Cornton Vale.

Mary lived with her mother throughout her upbringing, but at the age of 15 she began to abuse drugs and had contact with the Children's Panel for staying off school. When she was 16 she had a son and the bond between mother and son has always been particularly strong despite the unsettled circumstances of Mary's life. Thereafter Mary got into trouble with the police on a regular basis. When she was about 17, she began to abuse heroin. At the time of her apprehension, Mary was on a methadone prescription but was topping this up with heroin.

Mary invariably seemed to be happy enough in prison, to be coping satisfactorily with the difficulties of being in prison and to be getting on well with both fellow prisoners and staff at least in general terms. She had been on remand in Cornton Vale on at least two occasions. It seems that Mary knew from previous prison experience what to expect from Cornton Vale, was familiar with the rules and procedures, and may have known some of the inmates from previous incarcerations.

At the time of her custody, Gavin H., who was a life long friend of Mary, such that they were termed cousins, was in Greenock Prison. On 24 June 1998 Gavin H. hanged himself in Greenock Prison.

Mary's mother telephoned the prison in order that the news might be broken to her daughter. Mary was very distressed by this incident but appeared to cope within normal limits with such a deeply traumatic incident.

The funeral of Gavin H. was held on 3rd July 1998 and Mary was plainly upset on that date. Further, on that date she was expecting a visit from her sister and friend after they had attended Gavin H.'s funeral. The visitors arrived late but the visitor reception office contacted the remand block to see if Mary was available and was told that she was not in the remand block but had gone up to the football field to watch a game. This was in fact wrong. At that time, Mary was in her cell in the remand block, twinned up with another prisoner. When she realised she was not getting a visit because visiting hours were over, she was at first angry, throwing items about the cell. However, she appeared to settle down and about 2.30p.m. she arranged with her fellow prisoner that the duty officer should be called and that they should pretend to the staff that they had had an argument so that they could both be returned to their own cells. At about 3p.m. the duty officer brought Mary's cell mate back to the cell from the football match, when they found Mary in the wardrobe, suspended by a piece of electric flex round her neck.

Every attempt was made to revive her. She was taken to Stirling Royal Infirmary at 3.27p.m. Thereafter, after exhaustive attempts to revive her, she was pronounced dead at 8.57 the following morning.[161]

Determination by John Joseph Maguire, Queen's Counsel, Sheriff Principal of the Sheriffdom of Tayside Central and Fife in Fatal Accident Inquiry into the death of Mary Helen Pearson (otherwise Cowan), 10th December 1999.

NOTES

The documents are based mainly on the Transcript of Proceedings in the **Fatal Accident Inquiry** into the death of Angela Bollan and Others, which heard evidence in March and June 1997. The determination by John Joseph Maguire, Queen's Counsel, Sheriff Principal of Tayside and Fife was delivered on 18 November 1997.

The Fatal Accidents and Sudden Deaths Inquiry (Scotland) Act 1976 provides for the holding of public inquiries into, among other matters, the death of persons in legal custody.

Where the transcript is used as the source, FAI (Fatal Accident Inquiry) and the date of the evidence is given.

At times, the transcript is quoted verbatim, at others the evidence has been summarised into narrative, but the words used are always those of the person quoted. To facilitate reading, I have at times edited the advocates' and lawyers' questioning. For the same reason, I have not indicated Examination and Cross Examination.

Where the source stems from the Gilmour family, (interviews, or pre-cognitions given on behalf of the Gilmour family for the Inquiry, or documents, or evidence given at the Inquiry) *Gilmour* plus the relevant information is given.

Apart from members of the Gilmour family, names in the main body of the text have been changed.

PART ONE

[1] *Gilmour* Richard Gilmour, father.

[2] *Gilmour* Yvonne's sisters, Carolann and Michelle. Where their names appear in the main body of the text as sources, the extracts will not be referenced in the endnotes.

[3] *Gilmour* Extract from Yvonne's Social Enquiry Report, 30th August 1996

[4] Extract from Yvonne's Leverndale Discharge Summary 14th March 1996, quoted in FAI, 25th March 1997

[5] *Gilmour* Extract from Yvonne's Social Enquiry Report, 30th August 1996

[6] Extract from Yvonne's Leverndale Discharge Summary 14th March 1996, quoted in FAI, 25th March 1997

[7] *Gilmour* Extract from Yvonne's Social Enquiry Report, 30th August 1996

[8] Extract from Yvonne's Leverndale Discharge Summary 14th March 1996, quoted in FAI, 25th March 1997
[9] *Gilmour* From Yvonne's medical records.
[10] FAI 6th June 1997
[11] Extract from Yvonne's Leverndale Discharge Summary 14th March 1996, quoted in FAI, 25th March 1997
[12] Extract from Yvonne's Leverndale Discharge Summary 14th March 1996, quoted in FAI , 25th March 1997

PART TWO
[13] *Gilmour* Extracted from Yvonne's Charge Sheet for District Court of Glasgow (other names changed)
[14] *Gilmour* Extracted from Yvonne's medical records (except for Ruchill Hospital, all names of persons and places changed)
[15] *Gilmour* Extracted from Yvonne's medical records.
[16] FAI 25th March 1997, also for all following extracts in Chapter 3 except Medical Correpsondence.
[17] *Gilmour* Extracted from Yvonne's medical records. All other names changed.
[18] FAI 25th March 1997
[19] Unless otherwise stated, extracts in this section are based on *Gilmour* Precognitions taken on behalf of the Gilmour family and evidence from the FAI 25th March 1997
[20] Unless otherwise stated, extracts in the following section are taken from the FAI 26th March 1997.
[21] FAI 25th March 1997
[22] FAI 26h March 1997

PART THREE
[23] FAI 5th March 1997
[24] FAI 17th June 1997
[25] FAI 24th June 1997
[26] FAI 23rd June 1997
[27] FAI 23rd June 1997
[28] FAI 17th June 1997
[29] FAI 4th June 1997
[30] FAI 18th March 1997
[31] FAI 18th June 1997

32 FAI 24th June
33 FAI 16th and 17th June 1997
34 *Gilmour* Precognition taken on behalf of Gilmour family.
35 FAI 19th March 1997
36 FAI 19th June 1997
37 FAI 5th June 1997
38 FAI 23rd June 1997
39 FAI 24th March 1997
40 FAI 16th June 1997
41 FAI 17th June 1997
42 FAI 5th June 1997
43 FAI 23rd June 1997
44 FAI 24th March 1997
45 FAI 21st March 1997
46 FAI 17th March 1997
47 FAI 4th June 1997
48 FAI 24th March 1997
49 FAI 27th March 1997
50 FAI 17th March 1997
51 FAI 16th June 1997
52 FAI 16th June 1997
53 FAI 13th June 1997
54 FAI 16th June 1997
55 FAI 17th March 1997
56 FAI 5th June 1997
57 FAI 18th March 1997
58 FAI 17th June 1997
59 FAI 24th June 1997
60 FAI 10th March 1997
61 FAI 13th June 1997
62 FAI 25th March 1997
63 FAI 16th June 1997
64 FAI 17th June 1997
65 FAI 17th March 1997
66 FAI 24th March 1997
67 FAI 12th June 1997
68 From 'Suicide in Scottish Prisons 1976-93' in *The Journal of Forensic Psychiatry* Vol 6 No 3 December 1995, cited at FAI 11th June 1997.
69 FAI 24th June 1997

[70] FAI 24th June 1997
[71] FAI 18th March 1997
[72] FAI 16th June 1997
[73] FAI 24th June 1997
[74] FAI 11th June 1997
[75] FAI 4th June 1997
[76] FAI 11th June 1997
[77] FAI 17th March 1997
[78] FAI 21st March 1997
[79] FAI 24th June 1997
[80] FAI 21st March 1997
[81] FAI 6th June 1997
[82] FAI 19th June 1997
[83] FAI 24th March 1997
[84] FAI 21st March 1997
[85] FAI 13th June 1997
[86] FAI 16th June 1997
[87] FAI 2nd June 1997
[88] FAI 7th March 1997
[89] FAI 17th March 1997
[90] FAI 24th March 1997
[91] FAI 17th March 1997
[92] FAI 24th March 1997
[93] FAI 26th March 1997
[94] FAI 9th June 1997
[95] *Gilmour* From precognition taken on behalf of the Gilmour family for FAI.
[96] FAI 10th March 1997
[97] FAI 27th March 1997
[98] FAI 7th March 1997
[99] *Gilmour* From precognition taken on behalf of the Gilmour family for FAI.
[100] FAI 24th March 1997

PART FOUR

[101] FAI 26th March 1997
[102] FAI 2nd June 1997
[103] FAI 6th June 1997
[104] Letter from Yvonne to her girlfriend, cited FAI 11th June 1997

[105] FAI 10th March 1997
[106] This and the next four inmate statements: *Gilmour* From precognitions taken on behalf of the Gilmour family for the FAI.
[107] FAI 2nd June 1997
[108] This and the next inmate statement: *Gilmour* from precognitions taken on behalf of the Gilmour family for FAI.
[109] FAI 17th March 1997
[110] FAI 4th June 1997
[111] FAI 19th March 1997
[112] FAI 27th March 1997
[113] FAI 5th June 1997
[114] FAI 2nd June 1997
[115] FAI 24th June 1997
[116] FAI 10th June 1997
[117] Letter from Yvonne to her girlfriend. *Gilmour*.
[118] This and following inmate statement: *Gilmour* From precognition taken on behalf of the Gilmour family for FAI.
[119] FAI 19th March 1997
[120] FAI 17th March 1997
[121] FAI 2nd June 1997
[122] Letter from Yvonne to her girlfriend, *Gilmour*.
[123] Letter from Yvonne to her girlfriend, *Gilmour*
[124] This and following inmate statement: *Gilmour* from precognitions taken on behalf of the Gilmour family for FAI.
[125] Letter from Yvonne to her girlfriend in prison, quoted in FAI 27th March and 18th June 1997
[126] FAI 24th March 1997
[127] FAI 18th and 19th June 1997

PART FIVE

[128] This and following inmate statement: *Gilmour* From precognition taken on behalf of the Gilmour fanily for FAI.
[129] FAI 18th March 1997
[130] FAI 2nd and 3rd June 1997
[131] Cited FAI 10th June 1997
[132] FAI 4th June 1997
[133] This and next two extracts: *Gilmour* From precognitions taken on behalf of the Gilmour family for FAI.
[134] FAI 10th and 16th June 1997
[135] FAI 10th June 1997

[136] *Gilmour* From precognition taken on behalf of Gilmour family for FAI
[137] FAI 4th June 1997
[138] FAI 4th June 1997
[139] FAI 4th June 1997
[140] FAI 4th June 1997
[141] FAI 7th March 1997
[142] FAI 10th March 1997
[143] FAI 4th June 1997
[144] FAI 10th March 1997
[145] FAI 11th June 1997
[146] The title of the song is actually *Comfortably Numb* but in their statements and at the Inquiry the girls consistently refer to it as *Uncomfortably Numb*.
[147] FAI 7th and 10th March 1997.
[148] *Comfortably Numb* Words and Music by Roger Waters and David Gilmour © 1979 & 2000 Roger Waters Music Overseas Ltd/Pink Floyd Music Publishers Ltd (50%) Warner/Chappell Music Ltd, London W6 8BS. Text reproduced by kind permission of International Music Publications Ltd.
[149] FAI 7th March 1997
[150] FAI 19th March 1997
[151] FAI 7th and 10th March 1997
[152] FAI 19th March 1997
[153] FAI 4th June 1997
[154] FAI 19th March 1997
[155] FAI 5th June 1997
[156] FAI 7th and 10th March 1997
[157] FAI quoted 19th March 1997. Also Gilmour papers.

Some other books published by **LUATH** PRESS

CURRENT ISSUES

Scotland - Land and Power the agenda for land reform
Andy Wightman
ISBN 0 946487 70 7 PBK £5.00

Old Scotland New Scotland
Jeff Fallow
ISBN 0 946487 40 5 PBK £6.99

Notes from the North Incorporating a Brief History of the Scots and the English
Emma Wood
ISBN 0 946487 46 4 PBK £8.99

Some Assembly Required: behind the scenes at the rebirth of the Scottish Parliament
David Shepherd
ISBN 0 946487 84 7 PBK £7.99

POETRY

Poems to be read aloud
Collected and with an introduction by Tom Atkinson
ISBN 0 946487 00 6 PBK £5.00

Scots Poems to be Read Aloud
Collectit an wi an innin by Stuart McHardy
ISBN 0 946487 81 2 PBK £5.00

Blind Harry's Wallace
William Hamilton of Gilbertfield introduced by Elspeth King
ISBN 0 946487 43 X HBK £15.00
ISBN 0 946487 33 2 PBK £8.99

Men & Beasts
Valerie Gillies amd Rebecca Marr
ISBN 0 946487 92 8 PBK £15.00

The Luath Burns Companion
John Cairney
ISBN 1 84282 000 1 PBK £10.00

'Nothing but Heather!'
Gerry Cambridge
ISBN 0 946487 49 9 PBK £15.00

FICTION

But n Ben A-Go-Go
Matthew Fitt
ISBN 0 946487 82 0 HBK £10.99

Grave Robbers
Robin Mitchell
ISBN 0 946487 72 3 PBK £7.99

The Bannockburn Years
William Scott
ISBN 0 946487 34 0 PBK £7.95

The Great Melnikov
Hugh MacLachlan
ISBN 0 946487 42 1 PBK £7.95

FOLKLORE

Scotland: Myth Legend & Folklore
Stuart McHardy
ISBN 0 946487 69 3 PBK £7.99

The Supernatural Highlands
Francis Thompson
ISBN 0 946487 31 6 PBK £8.99

Tall Tales from an Island
Peter Macnab
ISBN 0 946487 07 3 PBK £8.99

Tales from the North Coast
Alan Temperley
ISBN 0 946487 18 9 PBK £8.99

ON THE TRAIL OF

On the Trail of John Muir
Cherry Good
ISBN 0 946487 62 6 PBK £7.99

On the Trail of Mary Queen of Scots
J. Keith Cheetham
ISBN 0 946487 50 2 PBK £7.99

On the Trail of William Wallace
David R. Ross
ISBN 0 946487 47 2 PBK £7.99

On the Trail of Robert Burns
John Cairney
ISBN 0 946487 51 0 PBK £7.99

On the Trail of Bonnie Prince Charlie
David R. Ross
ISBN 0 946487 68 5 PBK £7.99

On the Trail of Queen Victoria in the Highlands
Ian R. Mitchell
ISBN 0 946487 79 0 PBK £7.99

On the Trail of Robert the Bruce
David R. Ross
ISBN 0 946487 52 9 PBK £7.99

On the Trail of Robert Service
GW Lockhart
ISBN 0 946487 24 3 PBK £7.99

LUATH GUIDES TO SCOTLAND

Mull and Iona: Highways and Byways
Peter Macnab
ISBN 0 946487 58 8 PBK £4.95

South West Scotland
Tom Atkinson
ISBN 0 946487 04 9 PBK £4.95

The West Highlands: The Lonely Lands
Tom Atkinson
ISBN 0 946487 56 1 PBK £4.95

The Northern Highlands: The Empty Lands
Tom Atkinson
ISBN 0 946487 55 3 PBK £4.95

The North West Highlands: Roads to the Isles
Tom Atkinson
ISBN 0 946487 54 5 PBK £4.95

WALK WITH LUATH

Mountain Days & Bothy Nights
Dave Brown and Ian Mitchell
ISBN 0 946487 15 4 PBK £7.50

The Joy of Hillwalking
Ralph Storer
ISBN 0 946487 28 6 PBK £7.50

Scotland's Mountains before the Mountaineers
Ian Mitchell
ISBN 0 946487 39 1 PBK £9.99

LUATH WALKING GUIDES

Walks in the Cairngorms
Ernest Cross
ISBN 0 946487 09 X PBK £4.95

Short Walks in the Cairngorms
Ernest Cross
ISBN 0 946487 23 5 PBK £4.95

HISTORY

Reportage Scotland: History in the Making
Louise Yeoman
ISBN 0 946487 61 8 PBK £9.99

Edinburgh's Historic Mile
Duncan Priddle
ISBN 0 946487 97 9 PBK £2.99

SOCIAL HISTORY

Shale Voices
Alistair Findlay
foreword by Tam Dalyell MP
ISBN 0 946487 63 4 PBK £10.99
ISBN 0 946487 78 2 HBK £17.99

Crofting Years
Francis Thompson
ISBN 0 946487 06 5 PBK £6.95

A Word for Scotland
Jack Campbell
foreword by Magnus Magnusson
ISBN 0 946487 48 0 PBK £12.99

BIOGRAPHY

Tobermory Teuchter: A first-hand account of life on Mull in the early years of the 20th century
Peter Macnab
ISBN 0 946487 41 3 PBK £7.99

The Last Lighthouse
Sharma Kraustopf
ISBN 0 946487 96 0 PBK £7.99

Bare Feet and Tackety Boots
Archie Cameron
ISBN 0 946487 17 0 PBK £7.95

Come Dungeons Dark
John Taylor Caldwell
ISBN 0 946487 19 7 PBK £6.95

MUSIC AND DANCE

Highland Balls and Village Halls
GW Lockhart
ISBN 0 946487 12 X PBK £6.95

Fiddles & Folk: A celebration of the re-emergence of Scotland's musical heritage
GW Lockhart
ISBN 0 946487 38 3 PBK £7.95

FOOD AND DRINK

Edinburgh & Leith Pub Guide
Stuart McHardy
ISBN 0 946487 80 4 PBK £4.99

SPORT

Over the Top with the Tartan Army (Active Service 1992-97)
Andrew McArthur
ISBN 0 946487 45 6 PBK £7.99

Ski & Snowboard Scotland
Hilary Parke
ISBN 0 946487 35 9 PBK £6.99

Pilgrims in the Rough: St Andrews beyond the 19th hole
Michael Tobert
ISBN 0 946487 74 X PBK £7.99

CARTOONS

Broomie Law
Cinders McLeod
ISBN 0 946487 99 5 PBK £4.00

Luath Press Limited

committed to publishing well written books worth reading

LUATH PRESS takes its name from Robert Burns, whose little collie Luath (*Gael.*, swift or nimble) tripped up Jean Armour at a wedding and gave him the chance to speak to the woman who was to be his wife and the abiding love of his life. Burns called one of *The Twa Dogs* Luath after Cuchullin's hunting dog in *Ossian's Fingal*. Luath Press grew up in the heart of Burns country, and now resides a few steps up the road from Burns' first lodgings in Edinburgh's Royal Mile.

Luath offers you distinctive writing with a hint of unexpected pleasures.

Most UK and US bookshops either carry our books in stock or can order them for you. To order direct from us, please send a £sterling cheque, postal order, international money order or your credit card details (number, address of cardholder and expiry date) to us at the address below. Please add post and packing as follows: UK – £1.00 per delivery address; overseas surface mail – £2.50 per delivery address; overseas airmail – £3.50 for the first book to each delivery address, plus £1.00 for each additional book by airmail to the same address. If your order is a gift, we will happily enclose your card or message at no extra charge.

ILLUSTRATION: IAN KELLAS

Luath Press Limited
543/2 Castlehill
The Royal Mile
Edinburgh EH1 2ND
Scotland

Telephone: 0131 225 4326 (24 hours)
Fax: 0131 225 4324
email: gavin.macdougall@luath.co.uk
Website: www.luath.co.uk